The **250** Best
4-Ingredient
Recipes

Margaret Howard

Robert
ROSE

The 250 Best 4-Ingredient Recipes
Text copyright © 2002, 2009 Margaret Howard
Photographs copyright © 2002, 2009 Robert Rose Inc.
Cover and text design copyright © 2002, 2009 Robert Rose Inc.

For complete cataloguing information, see page 186.

Disclaimer
The recipes in this book have been carefully tested by our kitchen and our tasters. To the best of our knowledge, they are safe and nutritious for ordinary use and users. For those people with food or other allergies, or who have special food requirements or health issues, please read the suggested contents of each recipe carefully and determine whether or not they may create a problem for you. All recipes are used at the risk of the consumer.

We cannot be responsible for any hazards, loss or damage that may occur as a result of any recipe use.

For those with special needs, allergies, requirements or health problems, in the event of any doubt, please contact your medical adviser prior to the use of any recipe.

Design & Production: PageWave Graphics Inc.
Editor: Carol Sherman
Copy Editor: Deborah Aldcorn
Recipe Editor: Jennifer MacKenzie
Cover Photography: Colin Erricson
Cover Photo Food Stylist: Kathryn Robertson
Interior Photography: Mark T. Shapiro
Interior Photo Food Stylist: Kate Bush
Props Stylist: Charlene Erricson

The publisher and author wish to express their appreciation to the following supplier of props used in the food photography:

DISHES, LINENS AND ACCESSORIES

Homefront
371 Eglinton Ave. W.
Toronto, Ontario, M5N 1A3
Tel: (416) 488-3189
www.homefrontshop.com

FLATWARE

Gourmet Settings Inc.
245 West Beaver Creek Rd., Unit 10
Richmond Hill, Ontario, L4B 1L1
Tel: 1-800-551-2649
www.gourmetsettings.com

Cover image: Chicken and Peaches (page 90)

We acknowledge the financial support of the Government of Canada through the Book Publishing Industry Development Program (BPIDP) for our publishing activities.

Published by: Robert Rose Inc.
120 Eglinton Ave. E., Suite 800, Toronto, Ontario, Canada M4P 1E2
Tel: (416) 322-6552   Fax: (416) 322-6936

Printed in Canada
3 4 5 6 7 8 9 10   CP   15 14 13 12 11 10 09

CONTENTS

ACKNOWLEDGMENTS

THANK YOU TO MY PUBLISHER, BOB DEES, for his many reassuring phone calls and answers to my questions. To my husband and very best friend, John. He brings a calm to the confusion of the final days of my manuscripts and provides wise and helpful words as he assists me with his editorial comments. He also has very persevering taste buds.

To many friends who freely gave of their favorite four-ingredient recipes and my children who offered ongoing critical comments. To my son, Andrew and his wife, Rachael who always put their marketing minds to the task of titles and subtitles. Two special eleven-year-old granddaughters, Leah and Alana, while visiting during the summer of 2002, indulged Grandma by eating her many different foods. They freely offered suggestions while they ate as well as tested many of the dessert chapter recipes. To Carol Sherman, my editor, who many times challenged me on incomplete terminology, which has now made it a much more complete book.

Keith Medley, retired librarian and teacher for his research into the word "four." One evening in our living room, Keith commented, "There is something about the word four that I remember as being quite significant." And so he spent valuable time in the Robarts Library at University of Toronto in his quest for this meaning (if you are curious, see the Introduction for this information.)

Thank you to Andrew Smith, Joseph Gisini, Kevin Cockburn and Daniella Zanchetta of PageWave Graphics for the book design and layout. To food stylist Kate Bush, props stylist Charlene Erricson and food photographer Mark Shapiro. They've all contributed to making this book look so beautiful.

Many reference manuals, including *University of California, Berkeley Wellness Letter*, consumer magazines and the marketing boards and their current materials, were very helpful. *A Dictionary of Symbols*, second edition by J.E. Cirlot, Routledge & Kegan Paul, London, was the source for information on the word four. I especially find the *University of California Wellness Encyclopedia of Food and Nutrition* a very helpful book on all nutrition matters.

INTRODUCTION

IN CHOOSING THE TITLE FOR THIS BOOK, *The 250 Best 4-Ingredient Recipes*, I was curious to learn whether there is any special meaning to the word four.

I was indeed pleased to come across, with considerable help, the real significance of this word. It has far deeper meaning than 1, 2, 3, 4 in numerical order. There are four elements — earth (or solids), water (or liquids), air (or gas) and fire. There are four seasons — winter, spring, summer and fall. There are four points to the compass. There are four sides to the square. You will no doubt think of many other ways the word four or number 4 enters your life. I hope this book will be one of them.

In this book, I offer quick food preparation for the busy person who is not willing to compromise on great taste. The four-ingredient concept counts water, salt and pepper as non-ingredients. Everything else is an ingredient!

GETTING STARTED

Planning in all aspects of life is important no less so in meals. I suggest that the following points be considered with regard to meal planning. Unless stated otherwise, all recipes use large eggs and either 2% or homogenized milk.

- Be a planner by taking about 10 minutes to plan your dinners for the week. It's one of the best ways to ensure you place healthy dinners on the table even when you are in a hurry.

- Plan meals around main ingredients that cook quickly, such as fish, eggs, chicken breasts, cooked ham and turkey.

- Choose lots of fresh fruits and vegetables as support to the main ingredient.

- Choose main dishes that you can add to or alter to accommodate other ingredients. For example, when meat is the main dish, plan a side dish such as pasta that can be changed into a main entrée with the addition of beans, cheese, hard-cooked eggs or tofu.

- For budget supper solutions, choose inexpensive cuts of meat and meat alternatives that are both nutrient-packed and budget-friendly. Stretch meat and seafood by cooking them in pasta dishes, risottos, soups and stews.

- Plan one-pot meals such as stews, chilies or soups that are easily reheated in single-serving amounts.

- Use grains such as bulgur and couscous which, like rice and pasta, cook quickly.

- When necessary, use canned and frozen vegetables. They come out of the package ready to cook.

- Keep prepared sauces and spice mixtures on hand to add instant variety and flavor to your cooking.

- The microwave oven makes side dishes, such as rice, easier to prepare.

- By adding a new ingredient to your shopping list each week, you will soon have expanded your repertoire.

- Use quick-cooking methods such as broiling and grilling.

MEASURING UP!

Proper measuring is most important to the final results. For measuring butter, margarine and shortening, volume measure — not weight — is used most frequently in North America, whereas Europeans usually weigh. I have used volume in this book.

What is the correct way to measure? Measure liquid ingredients using glass or clear liquid-measuring cups. Measure dry ingredients using nested dry-measuring cups (usually made of plastic or metal) that can be leveled off with a knife. Measure flour by spooning — not scooping — it into dry measures and level off with a knife without shaking or tapping the cup.

GENERAL COOKING AND SELECTION TECHNIQUES

Fish and Seafood

A general rule of thumb: thin fish should be broiled, grilled, barbecued or microwaved; thick fish should be baked or poached.

Barbecuing, grilling and broiling are suitable for fatty fish such as salmon, trout and swordfish. Fish with less fat, such as sole, perch, red snapper, pickerel and cod, are best cooked in moist heat, such as microwaving or poaching.

Baking at a high temperature, approximately 450°F (230°C), is the ideal way to cook fish, especially whitefish and salmon.

When selecting fresh fish check the following:

- Eyes and gills must be bright, clear and bulging.

- Gills should be reddish or pink and fresh smelling.

- Scales should be shiny and tight to the skin.

- Fish should be firm and spring back when pressed.

- There should never be a strong or unpleasant odor.

Poultry

The following tips apply to all poultry, including chicken, duck, turkey and Rock Cornish hens.

Shopping Tips

1. Select packages that are cold and tightly wrapped without any tears or holes in the wrapping.
2. Do not buy poultry marked "previously frozen" unless you plan to cook it within one to three days.
3. Always check the label for the "best before" date.
4. Pick up any poultry at the end of your shopping along with other foods that require refrigeration or are frozen.
5. Ask the cashier to pack any fresh poultry (and meats) separately from the other items.

Storing and Hygiene Tips

1. Place packages at home in the coldest part of the refrigerator unless you are freezing them.
2. Immediately freeze any poultry you do not intend using within one to three days. Enclose packages in plastic freezer bags or overwrap in heavy-duty aluminum foil.
3. Washing poultry before cooking does not rinse off bacteria. Cooking thoroughly at high temperature does.
4. Wash hands thoroughly with soap and water before and after handling raw poultry.
5. Wash all utensils and surfaces with hot soapy water after preparing raw poultry to kill bacteria. Then sanitize with a solution of one part bleach to four parts water. Rinse well with cold water.
6. Do not let raw or cooked poultry stand at room temperature for longer than one hour.
7. When storing leftovers from roasted poultry, remove meat from bones and any stuffing from cavity.

Cooking Tips

1. Ground chicken and turkey have a softer texture than ground beef. For this reason, it is a good idea to add some fine dry bread crumbs and a beaten egg when making patties or meatballs. They will hold together better.
2. To keep ground patties moist, a small amount of sour cream, cranberry or tomato sauce is helpful.
3. Always marinate poultry in the refrigerator at all times of the year.
4. Reserve about $\frac{1}{4}$ cup (50 mL) marinade as a dipping sauce before placing poultry in the remaining marinade. After removing the poultry from the marinade, boil any leftover marinade for at least 5 minutes before brushing it on the poultry during cooking.

Meat and Pork

Safe Handling and Cooking Guidelines

Bacteria can be found on any raw meat products so it is essential we follow a few simple measures to protect the good health of those who dine at your table.

1. Food safety starts in the supermarket. Choose packages of meat that are cold and tightly wrapped and without tears or holes. Check labels for "best before" dates. Last day is fine. Pick up your meat at the end of your shopping trip and get it home and in the refrigerator as soon as possible.

2. Store meat in the refrigerator in plastic bags separated from other foods and positioned so that its juices cannot drip onto other foods. Meat cuts can be kept in a refrigerator set at 40°F (4°C) for one to three days. Freeze for longer storage. Keep ground meat no longer than one day in the refrigerator.

3. Thoroughly wash hands, utensils, cutting boards and work surfaces before, during and after handling raw meat. Use separate cutting boards for meat and for other foods.

4. Meat should be cooked until the proper internal temperature is achieved. Oven temperatures should be no lower than 250°F (120°C). Turn grilled meat cuts only once so that each side is seared. This ensures that bacteria, which occur only on the outside of the cut, are killed. It is safe to eat a cut of beef or veal cooked rare as long as the outside is seared.

5. Ground meat presents a particular food safety problem because any bacteria that may be on the surface of the raw meat will be mixed throughout the meat during grinding. It should never be consumed raw. It should always be thoroughly cooked until the internal temperature reaches 160°F (70°C).

6. Hot foods should be kept hot and separate from raw meat.

7. Never reuse marinade that was used to marinate raw meat unless it is brought to a boil for 5 minutes first. This will kill bacteria acquired from the raw meat.

8. Refrigerate leftovers within 2 hours of serving.

Government marketing agencies are making consumers lives much easier these days by providing information about meat products. This information includes cooking methods, proper storage and handling and nutritional values.

For guidance in roasting beef, the following may be of help:

DONENESS	INTERNAL TEMPERATURE	ROASTING TIME
Rare	140°F (60°C)	20 minutes per lb (500 g)
Medium	160°F (70°C)	25 minutes per lb (500 g)
Well	170°F (80°C)	30 minutes per lb (500 g)

Cuts recommended are prime rib, rib eye, tenderloin, strip loin and top sirloin.

> **Pork Facts and Figures**
> Through advances in breeding techniques and feeding, farmers have developed pork so lean that its fat content is close to that of a skinless chicken breast. According to the U.S. National Pork Board, some pork cuts have 31% less fat than they had just 20 years ago. In Canada, all fresh pork cuts, except ribs, contain less than 10% fat when trimmed of visible fat. It's easy to trim away extra fat as it is seen as a band around the outer edge of the meat.
>
> In the past, there has been a tendency to overcook pork. Current thinking is that pork should be cooked to medium 160°F (70°C) on an instant read thermometer with a hint of pink remaining. This maintains the natural succulent tenderness and flavor of pork while still safely killing any harmful bacteria. Remember to let roasts stand, loosely covered, for 10 minutes before slicing.

Salads

Here are a few simple rules that guarantee great green salads.

- Buy the freshest greens and buy frequently in order to have on hand the basics of a crisp pretty salad.

- Wash tenderly so as not to break the veins.

- Drain and pat dry or whirl dry in a salad spinner.

- Break or tear into bite-size pieces. Separate lettuce into quarters and then break apart.

- Chill the salad plates, platters or bowls before serving.

- Toss the salad ingredients and dressing just before serving.

- There is life after iceberg! Today's wonderful and vast range of greens include pungent arugula and endive, soft Boston and Bibb and peppery-tasting watercress. The darker the green, the more nutritious the vegetable is.

- For some creative garnishing ideas, repeat some of the ingredients that are in the salad. For example, Jellied Gazpacho (see recipe, page 51) looks great when garnished with thin cucumber twists (made like lemon twists) or green onion flowers. One word of caution — use vegetable garnishes for vegetable salads and fruit ones for fruit salads.

- Herbs and herb mixtures, such as tarragon, basil, thyme, oregano, rosemary and herbes de Provençe, add wonderful flavor to salads as well as dressings. Fresh is best but dried will do in a pinch. When substituting dried herbs for fresh, use one-third of the fresh amount. Your dried herbs should be fresh (discard those that are "over the hill"). Optimum period to store dry herbs is one year. Store in a dark cupboard away from heat, light and moisture.

Vegetables

Cooking Tips

No matter how you cook your vegetables, the following tips apply.

1. Do not salt vegetables while steaming, microwave-cooking, baking or pan-frying. Salt draws liquid from the vegetables, causing them to cook unevenly. This does not apply to boiling vegetables.

2. Cutting or chopping vegetables that are high in vitamin C releases an enzyme that can destroy the vitamin. To retain the most vitamin C, leave all vegetables whole or in as large pieces as possible until you are ready to eat them.

3. Roasting adds a certain seductive quality to many vegetables. The best candidates are those with lots of flavor and fiber, such as potatoes, beets, peppers, squash, carrots, parsnips and onions. Asparagus and tomatoes are newcomers to the roasting scene. Tossing the veggies with a little oil to lightly coat prevents them from drying out. Roast, uncrowded, on a baking sheet at high temperature, around 425°F (220°C). This technique can also be used on a barbecue grill.

Microwaving Vegetables

Vegetables as well as fruits retain more nutrients when cooked in a microwave than when they are boiled, steamed or baked. To get the most from your microwave oven:

1. Add as little water as possible to the food — 1 tsp (5 mL) is just enough. Ideally, no water should be left at the end of cooking.

2. Defrost foods in the microwave — they'll retain more nutrients than those defrosted in the refrigerator because there is less time for nutrients to degrade.

3. Always cover foods while cooking in the microwave. This reduces both cooking time and nutrient loss.

4. Cook at High power. Again, the quicker foods cook, the more nutrients they retain.

5. Don't overcook. Let foods stand afterward for 5 minutes to finish heating since microwave-cooked foods cook from the outside in.*

*University of California, Berkeley Wellness Letter, February, 2002

APPETIZERS & BEVERAGES

APPETIZERS HAVE THE JOYFUL RESPONSIBILITY OF SETTING THE STAGE, warming up the audience and teasing the palette. Whether piping hot or chilled to icy perfection, appetizers are the delicate fore tastes that beguile the senses and promise more good flavors to follow. They should be served in quantities to tempt, but not to fill. The edge has been taken off many a fine dinner because the appetizers were too many and too much.

Whether for dunking or spreading, nibbling or noshing, our appetizers make any gathering memorable. Some team up with crudités, chips, crackers and pita pieces while others make it on their own. There are cheesy concoctions, pâtés, seafood delicacies and appetizing dips. Some can be prepared ahead and stored frozen or refrigerated for busy days. Others require more last-minute preparation. And some may also be useful for lunches or late-evening snacks.

SHRIMP PUFFS

Here's a different perspective on an open-face sandwich — baked until puffed and golden brown. Make the shrimp mixture ahead and refrigerate. When you're ready, spread it on bread and then toast it in the oven.

Makes 24 puffs		

• PREHEAT OVEN TO 375°F (190°C)

6	slices white sandwich bread	6
I	can (3.75 oz/106 g) shrimp, drained	I
½ cup	light mayonnaise	125 mL
I	green onion, chopped	I
	Salt and freshly ground black pepper	

1. Trim crusts from bread. Cut each slice into four triangles.

2. In a small bowl, mash shrimp with mayonnaise and onion. Season with salt and pepper to taste.

3. Spread mixture evenly on bread triangles. Bake on pan in preheated oven for 10 minutes or until puffed and golden brown. Serve warm.

SARDINE LOVER'S PÂTÉ

Even non-sardine lovers will enjoy this tangy lemon sardine pâté on a plain cracker or thin baguette slice.

Makes ⅔ cup (150 mL)		

I	can (3.75 oz/106 g) sardines, drained	I
¼ cup	light sour cream	50 mL
½ tsp	lemon zest	2 mL
I tbsp	freshly squeezed lemon juice	15 mL

1. In a food processor, combine sardines, sour cream, lemon zest and juice. Pulse with on/off motion until mixture is almost smooth.

2. Store in a covered container in refrigerator for up to one week or freeze for longer storage.

RED PEPPER AIOLI

This excellent dip is based on aioli, the garlic-flavored mayonnaise of Provence. Adding roasted red peppers to the basic recipe makes a fabulous dip for raw vegetables. Or use it as you would regular mayonnaise.

Makes 1 cup (250 mL)			
3	cloves garlic		3
½ cup	light mayonnaise		125 mL
1	jar (12 oz/370 mL) roasted red peppers, well drained		1
¼ tsp	hot pepper flakes		1 mL
	Salt and freshly ground black pepper		

1. In a food processor with motor running, drop garlic through chute and process until finely minced.

2. Add mayonnaise, red peppers and hot pepper flakes. Process until almost smooth. Season with salt and pepper to taste.

3. Store in a covered container in refrigerator for up to one week or freeze for longer storage.

MEXICANA NACHO DIP

This easy, fast and simply delicious appetizer is always a big success at any get-together. The bright Mexican colors make it particularly attractive. Serve it with nacho chips and raw vegetables.

Serves 6		
1 cup	light sour cream (see Tip, left)	250 mL
1	medium tomato, diced	1
1	green onion, chopped	1
½ cup	shredded Cheddar cheese	125 mL

TIP
Sour cream has about 6 grams of fat and 60 calories in 2 tbsp (25 mL). Nonfat sour cream has virtually no fat, of course, and only 20 to 35 calories.

1. Spread sour cream evenly over bottom of a shallow serving dish.

2. Top with tomato, green onion and cheese. Cover and refrigerate for several hours until ready to serve.

ROASTED PEAR WITH BRIE CHEESE

Roasted pears put a new twist on baked Brie cheese to make this a favorite cocktail munchy. It goes especially well with freshly sliced baguette.

• PREHEAT OVEN TO 425°F (220°C)

Serves 8

1	6-inch (15 cm) round Brie cheese	1
1 tbsp	melted butter or margarine	15 mL
2	ripe pears, peeled and thinly sliced	2
1 tsp	chopped fresh thyme or $\frac{1}{2}$ tsp (2 mL) dried thyme	5 mL

1. Remove top rind from cheese and discard.

2. Brush a baking sheet with melted butter. Arrange pear slices on sheet. Roast in preheated oven for 15 minutes. Turn slices and roast for 10 minutes more or until edges are caramelized. Let cool.

3. Top cheese with pears, overlapping slices and refrigerate (for up to 4 hours) until ready to bake.

4. Just before serving, heat cheese and pears in 350°F (180°C) oven for 10 minutes or until cheese is softened. Sprinkle with thyme and serve.

SUN-DRIED TOMATO CHEESE SPREAD

Wonderful flavorful things happen when you combine cream cheese with sun-dried tomatoes. Use as a spread on crackers or sliced baguette.

Makes 1$\frac{1}{2}$ cups (375 mL)

1	package (8 oz/250 g) light or regular cream cheese, softened	1
$\frac{1}{2}$ cup	butter or margarine, softened	125 mL
$\frac{1}{2}$ cup	freshly grated Parmesan cheese	125 mL
$\frac{1}{2}$ cup	chopped oil-packed sun-dried tomatoes, drained	125 mL

1. In a food processor or bowl using an electric mixer, beat cheese and butter until smooth. Stir in Parmesan cheese and tomatoes.

2. Transfer to a small bowl. Cover and refrigerate before serving. Return to room temperature for easy spreading.

3. Store in a covered container in refrigerator for up to one week or freeze for longer storage.

"ENDS OF CHEESE" SPREAD

In one of those sudden bursts of clean-up frenzy, I noticed many small amounts of cheese lurking in resealable bags in the refrigerator. Putting them together in the food processor with some antipasto produced this tasty spread.

Makes 1 cup (250 mL)		
½	package (8 oz/250 g) light cream cheese	½
½ cup	commercial or homemade antipasto (see Tip, left)	125 mL
½ cup	shredded assorted cheeses (see Tip, left)	125 mL
1 to 2 tsp	Worcestershire sauce	5 to 10 mL

TIPS

Use a salsa rather than antipasto for a change of flavor.

Any number of different hard or soft cheeses will work in this spread, but it is a good idea to have some cream cheese for a nice spreading consistency. Add hot sauce or cayenne pepper for an extra bit of "heat."

1. In a food processor, combine cream cheese, antipasto and shredded cheeses.

2. Pulse with on/off motion until mixture is blended but not completely smooth. Stir in Worcestershire sauce to taste.

3. Transfer to a small bowl. Cover and refrigerate until chilled before serving. Store in a covered container in refrigerator for up to one week or freeze for longer storage.

SWISS CHEESE PÂTÉ

Mellow Swiss cheese adds "upmarket" appeal to a pâté. Sitting for a day or so allows time for flavors to mellow. Serve with sliced apples or pears, crackers or thinly sliced baguette.

Serves 6 to 8		
½ cup	whipping (35%) cream	125 mL
1	clove garlic	1
1 cup	shredded Swiss cheese	250 mL
¼ tsp	freshly ground nutmeg	1 mL

1. In a small saucepan over medium heat, heat cream and garlic just until cream comes to a boil. Remove from heat and discard garlic.

2. Slowly add cheese, stirring after each addition, until cheese has melted. Stir in nutmeg.

3. Transfer to a small serving bowl. Cover and refrigerate until firm.

4. Remove from refrigerator one hour before serving time. It can be served warm or at room temperature.

HOT SALSA CHEESE DIP

This delicious appetizer is great served with corn nacho chips.

Serves 12

TIP
To prevent avocado from browning, sprinkle with a little lime or lemon juice.

• PREHEAT OVEN TO 350°F (180°C)
• 9-INCH (2.5 L) SQUARE OR (23 CM) ROUND BAKING DISH

2 cups	mild or medium salsa	500 mL
1 lb	Monterey Jack cheese, cubed	500 g
1	avocado, peeled and diced	1
2 tbsp	chopped fresh cilantro	25 mL

1. Spread salsa in bottom of baking dish. Top with cheese cubes.

2. Bake in preheated oven for 25 minutes or until cheese melts and salsa is heated. Remove from oven. Top with avocado and cilantro. Serve warm.

TAPENADE

This superb appetizer is an olive lover's dream come true. It comes to us from Provence. Tapenade is a very traditional purée of black olives with capers, anchovies, garlic and, frequently, olive oil. It is spread on crusty bread or crackers, alone or "married" with cream or chèvre cheese. I use it in Tapenade Vinaigrette and Tapenade Mayonnaise (see recipes, page 66), Mediterranean Chicken (see recipe, page 89) or add some to sour cream or yogurt for a lighter dip for raw vegetables. I also add it to a tomato sauce to toss with pasta to give extra special flavor.

Makes 1 cup (250 mL)

1 cup	pitted black olives (see Tips, left)	250 mL
3	flat anchovy fillets	3
2 tbsp	drained capers	25 mL
1 to 3	cloves garlic (see Tips, left)	1 to 3
	Water or lemon juice	
	Freshly ground black pepper	

TIPS

You can use a cherry pitter to remove olive pits, but proper olive pitters are well worth the investment, if you do a lot of pitting. They are available in gourmet shops and many hardware stores. Otherwise, place a few olives on a flat cutting surface. Give them a good whack with the wide flat side of the blade of a heavy chef's knife. The olives will pop open, exposing the pits for easy removal.

Vary the amount of garlic according to your personal preference.

Because the purée is very thick, water will thin it but olive oil is more traditional.

1. In a food processor, pulse olives, anchovies, capers and garlic with on/off motion to a finely chopped paste.

2. The mixture will be very thick, so add a small amount of water, lemon juice or oil (see Tip, left). Season with pepper to taste. Tapenade keeps very well in the refrigerator for several weeks and can be frozen.

SERVING SUGGESTION

Hummus Tapenade Appetizer

- Spread hummus in bottom of a shallow round serving dish. Spread Tapenade in a small circle over center of hummus. Chop a firm tomato into small pieces. Scatter around outer edge of hummus. Serve with crackers or soft pita pieces.

ARTICHOKE CAPONATA SPREAD

We have enjoyed eating caponata, a Sicilian side dish or relish, on many occasions. Initially, it was whenever our friends Mary and Dave brought us a container from their favorite Italian store. But alas, this was not frequent enough to satisfy our tastes, so I was forced to reproduce it. Here is my version of this great spread. Serve it with toast, crackers or raw vegetables. But Homemade Crostinis are the best (see recipe below).

Makes 2 cups (500 mL)

TIP
It is becoming easier to find Asiago cheese in many supermarkets. In fact, I have found it already shredded, which truly makes fast work of this spread.

• PREHEAT OVEN TO 350°F (180°C)

1	can (14 oz/398 mL) water-packed artichokes, drained	1
1 cup	shredded Asiago cheese (see Tip, left)	250 mL
½ cup	light mayonnaise or plain low-fat yogurt	125 mL
1 to 2	cloves garlic	1 to 2
	Freshly ground black pepper	

1. In a food processor, process artichokes until coarsely chopped. Add cheese, mayonnaise and garlic. Pulse with on/off motion until mixture is almost smooth. Season with pepper to taste.

2. Store in a covered container in refrigerator for up to one week or freeze for longer storage.

3. Bake in preheated oven in a small casserole for 20 minutes or until hot, just before serving. Or serve cold — it is delicious either way.

HOMEMADE CROSTINIS

• Cut a crusty baguette into twenty-four ½-inch (1 cm) thick slices. Brush both sides lightly with olive oil. Arrange on a baking sheet. Bake in 350°F (180°C) oven for 15 minutes or until lightly toasted.

CHICKPEA DIP

Often called hummus, this high-fiber vegetarian dip is of Middle Eastern origin. Vegetables or soft pita bread are great for dipping. Cumin, if you like it, makes the dip more authentic.

Makes 2¹⁄₃ cups (575 mL)

TIP
I usually freeze some of the dip in smaller amounts so it can be used later as a sandwich spread or dip.

1	can (19 oz/540 mL) chickpeas, drained	1
1 to 2	cloves garlic, minced	1 to 2
½ cup	plain yogurt or light mayonnaise	125 mL
2 tbsp	freshly squeezed lemon juice	25 mL
½ tsp	salt	2 mL
	Freshly ground black pepper	

1. In a food processor or blender, process chickpeas with garlic until coarsely chopped. Add yogurt, lemon juice, salt and pepper. Process to a smooth paste.
2. Store in a covered container in the refrigerator for at least 2 hours so the flavor can develop.

BRANDIED CHEESE SPREAD

It's best to let this spread rest for a few days before serving so the flavors can mellow. Serve it with a variety of different crackers.

Makes 2 cups (500 mL)

Variation
Dry sherry or port is a pleasant change from brandy.

½ cup	butter or margarine, softened	125 mL
3 cups	shredded old Cheddar cheese	750 mL
2 tbsp	brandy (see Variation, left)	25 mL
1 tbsp	sesame seeds	15 mL

1. In a food processor, combine butter, cheese, brandy and sesame seeds. Pulse with on/off motion until smooth.
2. Transfer to a small bowl. Cover and refrigerate before serving. Store in a covered container in refrigerator for up to one week or freeze for longer storage.
3. Return to room temperature for easy spreading.

POLENTA PIE

Pesto sauce and polenta, the great cornmeal comfort food from northern Italy, make this an interesting and typical Italian recipe.

Makes 18 pieces

TIP
To serve six for a vegetarian lunch, use a 9-inch (23 cm) greased pie plate instead of the square pan. Then cut the pie into small wedges.

- PREHEAT OVEN TO 350°F (180°C)
- 9-INCH (2.5 L) SQUARE BAKING PAN, LIGHTLY GREASED

1	roll (1 lb/500 g) polenta	1
1 cup	finely chopped tomatoes	250 mL
½ cup	Basil Pesto Sauce (see recipe, page 132) or store-bought	125 mL
1 cup	shredded Mozzarella cheese	250 mL

1. Slice polenta into 18 thin slices. Arrange nine in prepared pan, overlapping if necessary.

2. Distribute tomatoes evenly over polenta. Top with dollops of pesto.

3. Top with remaining polenta slices and press down. Sprinkle with cheese.

4. Bake in preheated oven for 15 minutes or until polenta is heated through and cheese is melted.

5. To serve, cut into 18 small pieces and serve as finger food or in larger pieces for lunch.

GOAT CHEESE MUFFULETTAS

The magic ingredient is goat cheese, also known as chèvre. It is a white cheese with a delightfully tart flavor that easily distinguishes it from other cheeses.

Makes 30 pieces

TIP
You can also use peppers that you have roasted yourself (see Grilled Vegetables, page 146, for directions).

1	French baguette	1
½ cup	Tapenade (see recipe, page 17) or store-bought	125 mL
1	jar (8 oz/212 g) roasted red peppers, drained (see Tip, left)	1
5 oz	soft goat cheese	150 g
	Fresh basil leaves (optional)	

Pesto Variation
For a different muffuletta, replace Tapenade with Pesto.

1. Cut bread lengthwise in half. Remove some of the soft center from each half.

2. Thinly spread Tapenade on each cut side. Top with red pepper pieces, then thin slices of goat cheese. Add as many basil leaves as are needed to cover the cheese. Top with second half to form a sandwich.

3. Wrap tightly with plastic wrap. Refrigerate for several hours or overnight. Unwrap and cut into thin slices. Arrange slices in a spoke pattern on a round serving platter.

FESTIVE WARM BRIE

Here are three different toppings to try for this holiday favorite. Choose whichever you prefer — all offer different flavors — and all are very colorful.

Serves 6

Variations

Tomato Topping
Stir together 1/4 cup (50 mL) seeded and finely chopped tomato, 1 small minced garlic clove, 1/2 tsp (2 mL) olive oil and salt and pepper.

Strawberry Topping
Stir together 1/2 cup (125 mL) chopped strawberries, 2 tbsp (25 mL) slivered almonds and 2 tbsp (25 mL) sweet sherry.

• *PREHEAT OVEN TO 350°F (180°C)*
• *RIMMED BAKING SHEET, FOIL-LINED*

I	Brie or Camembert cheese, about 4-inches (10 cm) diameter	I
¼ cup	finely chopped red bell pepper	50 mL
I tbsp	finely chopped jalapeño pepper	15 mL
I	small clove garlic, minced	I

1. Remove top rind from cheese and discard. Place on prepared baking sheet.

2. Stir together peppers and garlic (see Variations, left, for other toppings). Spoon over cheese. Can be covered and refrigerated for up to half a day.

3. Bake in preheated oven for 10 minutes or until cheese starts to melt. Serve immediately with crackers such as water biscuits.

PROVOLONE CHEESE TOASTS

Delicious and always popular, these cheese toasts are fast and easy to make. Any good melting cheese can be used but Provolone does give that special Italian taste.

Makes 16 slices		

TIP
A French baguette is best when fresh. To keep it from becoming stale, slice to desired thickness and freeze in a tightly sealed plastic bag. When thawed, the baguette slices will still be bakery fresh.

• *PREHEAT BROILER*

8 oz	Provolone cheese, thinly sliced	250 g
I	French baguette, sliced into 16 thick slices (see Tip, left)	I
	Dried or fresh basil or oregano leaves	
	Chopped fresh parsley	

1. Cut cheese slices to fit bread slices. Set aside.
2. Place bread on baking pan and broil until golden brown. Remove pan from oven and turn bread slices over. Arrange cheese on top. Sprinkle lightly with herbs.
3. Return bread to broiler. Broil until cheese is melted. Serve at once while still warm.

PESTO TOASTS

Pesto Toasts make an excellent appetizer or accompaniment to soup. Keep them in the freezer for last-minute occasions.

Makes 20 slices		

TIP
Pesto is available at either the refrigerated deli counter in supermarkets or the imported foods section.

• *PREHEAT BROILER*

I	French baguette, cut into 20 thin slices	I
¼ cup	light mayonnaise	50 mL
¼ cup	Basil Pesto Sauce (see recipe, page 132) or store-bought (see Tip, left)	50 mL
2 tbsp	grated Asiago cheese	25 mL

1. Place bread on a baking sheet. Set aside.
2. In a small bowl, combine mayonnaise, pesto and cheese. Spread a small amount on each bread slice.
3. Broil for 3 minutes or until cheese and edges of bread are browned.

TZATZIKI

In Greece, the word for appetizer is mezé. Tzatziki is a light and refreshing mezé that is almost always served before a Greek meal. Adjust the garlic "hit" to suit your personal taste. The best tzatziki is made with drained yogurt, often referred to as yogurt cheese. Serve with crackers, pita pieces or pita chips (see recipe below).

<table>
<tr><td colspan="3">Makes 2 cups
(500 mL)</td></tr>
</table>

2 cups	plain yogurt (see Tip, left)	500 mL
I	small seedless cucumber, unpeeled, grated (about 2 cups/500 mL grated)	I
2	small cloves garlic, crushed	2
I tbsp	chopped fresh dill	15 mL
	Salt and freshly ground black pepper	

TIPS

Check labels when choosing plain yogurt to make yogurt cheese. Be sure to choose a brand without gelatin, starch or gums, as they will not drain.

Whey from drained yogurt can be used as extra liquid in soups or stews. As well, it contains B vitamins and minerals.

Yogurt cheese is also great for spreads, salad dressings, cream cheese replacement and on baked potatoes. I frequently use it as a low-fat replacement for whipped cream. Folded into a dessert mixture, it maintains a good texture and does not break down.

1. *Yogurt Cheese:* Line a sieve with cheesecloth or a paper coffee filter set over a medium-size bowl. Spoon yogurt into sieve. Cover and refrigerate for several hours or overnight. Then, gather edges of cheesecloth together and gently squeeze out any remaining whey liquid (see Tip, left). (You should have about 1 cup/250 mL cheese.) Transfer to a bowl.

2. Drain and squeeze liquid from cucumber with your hands. Stir cucumber, garlic and dill into yogurt cheese. Season with salt and pepper to taste. Cover and refrigerate until ready to serve. Stir just before serving. Tzatziki keeps well refrigerated for up to one week.

PITA CHIPS

- Cut 4 (6-inch/15 cm) pita breads into 8 wedges each. Brush lightly with olive oil. Bake on a baking sheet in a 350°F (180°C) oven for 5 minutes or until crisp. Allow to cool then store in a plastic bag. Makes 32 pieces.

MUSHROOM CHEESE PÂTÉ

Make this wonderful pâté anytime you have an abundance of mushrooms on hand. Add a sprinkling of chopped fresh parsley for color.

Makes 2½ cups (625 mL)		
1 lb	button mushrooms or a variety of mixed mushrooms	500 g
2 tbsp	butter or margarine	25 mL
1½ cups	shredded Cheddar cheese	375 mL
1 tbsp	horseradish	15 mL

1. Coarsely chop mushrooms. Set aside.

2. In a nonstick skillet on high heat, melt butter. Add mushrooms and cook, stirring frequently, for 5 minutes or until mushrooms are softened and liquid has evaporated. Set aside to cool slightly.

3. Place mushrooms in a food processor and process until fairly smooth. Add cheese and process again until smooth. Add horseradish to taste. Transfer to a small bowl. Cover and refrigerate until chilled before serving. Store in a covered container in refrigerator for up to one week or freeze for longer storage.

FRESH FRUIT SMOOTHIE

What a great chance to have your antioxidants in a glass! This delicious smoothie can be a real morning or middle of the day "power" drink.

Serves 1		
¾ cup	plain or vanilla yogurt	175 mL
½ cup	sliced fresh or frozen strawberries	125 mL
½	ripe banana	½
¼ cup	apple or orange juice	50 mL

Variation
Banana Split Smoothie
Replace yogurt with chocolate milk. Use 1 large banana and no strawberries.

1. In a blender or food processor, process yogurt, strawberries, banana and juice until very smooth.

2. Pour contents into a tall chilled glass and enjoy!

CITRUS BUBBLY

Vitamins with your bubbly make this the perfect drink
to turn breakfast or brunch into a celebration.

Serves 4 to 6	• FLUTED CHAMPAGNE GLASSES	
4	large seedless oranges	4
⅓ cup	granulated sugar	75 mL
I	bottle (26 oz/750 mL) chilled sparkling wine or Champagne	I
	Sliced strawberries	

1. Remove peel in large strips from 1 orange.
2. In a small saucepan, bring orange strips, ¾ cup (175 mL) water and sugar to a boil. Simmer, uncovered, for 5 minutes. Remove from heat and let cool. Strain and discard orange strips.
3. Squeeze juice from 4 oranges to measure 3 cups (750 mL).
4. Pour sugar mixture and juice into a large pitcher. Add wine and pour into fluted glasses. Serve with strawberries.

KIR ROYALE

The basic ingredients are simple for this very festive drink — chilled Champagne
and Crème de Cassis, a liqueur made from the European black currant. Kir is
usually served as an apéritif and in France "vin ordinaire" may be used.
The cassis can mask the taste of a wine that is a touch too "ordinaire."

Serves 6	• FLUTED CHAMPAGNE GLASSES	
¼ cup	chilled Crème de Cassis	50 mL
I	bottle (26 oz/750 mL) chilled Champagne	I

Variation
Replace the Champagne with an equivalent amount of chilled dry sparkling white wine.

1. Place a small amount, or as the French would say "a soupçon," of cassis in each fluted glass. Fill with Champagne and serve immediately.

WHITE WINE SPANISH SANGRIA

Sangria is commonly made with red wine. This version uses
white wine with peach and lime slices for a lighter, summery taste.

Makes 6 cups (1.5 L)		
½ cup	granulated sugar	125 mL
1	peach, peeled and thinly sliced	1
1	lime, thinly sliced	1
1	bottle (26 oz/750 mL) dry white wine	1

TIP
If desired, sparkling water may be added to taste to the pitcher.

Red Wine Variation
Replace white wine with red wine and use thinly sliced oranges or apples instead of peaches and lime.

1. In a saucepan, bring sugar and 1 cup (250 mL) water to a boil, stirring until sugar is dissolved. Cool syrup to room temperature. Place peach and lime slices in bowl and pour syrup over. Chill for 4 hours or longer.

2. Fill a large pitcher with ice. Add wine, fruit and syrup. Stir gently to mash fruit with a wooden spoon.

3. Serve sangria in wineglasses with 1 or 2 slices of fruit per glass.

IRISH COFFEE

An Irish chef created this drink for passengers who had made
an emergency landing at an Irish airport. It was then passed along to
a bartender from San Francisco's old Buena Vista Hotel.

Serves 2		
½ cup	chilled whipping (35%) cream	125 mL
4 tsp	granulated sugar	20 mL
3 oz	Irish whiskey, divided	90 mL
	Hot strong coffee	

1. In a small bowl, whip cream with sugar until it just holds stiff peaks.

2. Divide whiskey between two large coffee mugs. Fill three-quarters full with hot coffee and top each mug with a large dollop of whipped cream.

SOUPS

SOUPS HAVE BEEN POPULAR AROUND THE WORLD FOR CENTURIES. THEY nourish the body and invigorate the soul. They have a special welcome-home quality, whether as a light prelude to a dinner or a hearty main course. Cold soup can be a refreshing entrée on a hot summer day. Hearty main-course hot soups give us time-saving and budget-stretching meals.

Our selection of recipes includes a taste journey of world soups. Starting in Russia (or any part of Eastern Europe), we sample a cabbage and beet borscht, served with a dollop of sour cream and fresh rye bread. Moving to Italy, we enjoy a pasta fagioli from the Tuscany region. On to Spain, for its famous garlic soup. Then to Greece, for avgolemono, a chicken soup with rice, eggs and lots of lemon. And finally northern Africa, to savor a Moroccan lentil soup, a vegetarian chickpea and lentil soup. Enjoy a "geography lesson in a bowl."

The remaining soups could come from anywhere and they simply reflect my notion of interesting and good-tasting soups. All the soups in this chapter are nutritious and faster than you might think to prepare.

TARRAGON BEET SOUP

This soup is excellent, considering how easy it is to make. A dollop of sour cream along with a sprig of fresh tarragon provides a nice garnish.

Makes 4 cups (1 L), about 3 servings		
I	can (14 oz/398 mL) sliced beets, including juice	I
2 cups	beef stock (see Tip, left)	500 mL
I tsp	red wine vinegar	5 mL
I tsp	chopped fresh tarragon or ¼ tsp (I mL) dried	5 mL
	Salt and freshly ground black pepper	

TIP
Use either beef bouillon cubes or canned beef broth diluted according to label. Since both are usually quite salty, be sure to taste before adding any additional salt.

1. In a medium saucepan over high heat, bring beets with juice and stock to a boil. Reduce heat, cover and cook for 5 minutes.

2. Remove from heat. Cool slightly before puréeing in a food processor or blender with vinegar and tarragon until smooth.

3. Return to saucepan and reheat to serving temperature. Season with salt and pepper to taste.

PASTA FAGIOLI SOUP

This Tuscan soup is a cinch to make when you use Basic Tomato Red Sauce.

Makes 6 cups (1.5 L), about 5 servings		
2 cups	Basic Red Tomato Sauce (see recipe, page 120) or store-bought	500 mL
I	can (19 oz/540 mL) cooked white beans, drained and rinsed	I
½ cup	elbow macaroni	125 mL
	Salt and freshly ground black pepper	
	Freshly grated Parmesan cheese	

1. In a large saucepan over high heat, bring tomato sauce, $1\frac{1}{2}$ cups (375 mL) water (adding more as necessary), drained beans and macaroni to a boil. Reduce heat. Cover and cook slowly, stirring often, for 20 minutes or until pasta is tender but firm.

2. Season with salt and pepper to taste. Serve in warm soup bowls garnished with cheese.

CABBAGE BEET BORSCHT

Borscht is a Russian and Eastern European soup dominated by the sweet taste of beets. It may also contain other vegetables and meat or meat broth. This version of traditional borscht takes just minutes to prepare.

	Makes 3 cups (750 mL), about 2 servings	
2 cups	shredded cabbage	500 mL
1	can (14 oz/398 mL) sliced beets, including juice	1
2 cups	beef stock (see Tip, page 28)	500 mL
1	small onion, chopped	1
	Salt and freshly ground black pepper	

TIP
After cooling soup and puréeing, it may be chilled and frozen for future use. Chilled Borscht is one of the world's great cold soups.

1. In a medium saucepan over high heat, bring cabbage, beets with juice, stock and onion to a boil. Reduce heat, cover and cook slowly for 20 minutes or until cabbage is soft.

2. Remove from heat. Cool slightly before puréeing in a food processor or blender until smooth (see Tip, left).

3. Return to saucepan and reheat to serving temperature. Season with salt and pepper to taste.

SERVING SUGGESTION

- Add a dollop of sour cream and a splash of vinegar just before serving for authenticity as well as taste.

TOMATO BISQUE

Generally, a bisque-style soup is thick and rich, frequently consisting of puréed seafood and cream. This version is made without cream and yet tastes fabulous. Its creamy character comes from puréeing all or a portion of the vegetables with the stock in which they are cooked. For maximum flavor, make the soup the day before and reheat it at serving time.

Makes 6 cups (1.5 L), about 5 servings

TIP
Any vegetable can be puréed in its cooking water to produce a creamy-textured soup without the cream. The starchier the vegetable, the creamier the resulting soup.

3 cups	chicken or vegetable stock	750 mL
½ cup	finely chopped onion	125 mL
I	can (19 oz/398 mL) tomatoes	I
⅓ cup	red wine or stock	75 mL
	Salt and freshly ground black pepper	

1. In a large saucepan over high heat, bring stock and onions to a boil. Add tomatoes and wine. Reduce heat, cover and cook slowly for 25 minutes.

2. Remove from heat. Cool slightly before puréeing half of soup in a food processor or blender until almost smooth. Repeat with remaining soup. Return to saucepan.

3. Reheat to serving temperature or refrigerate for up to 2 days and then reheat. Season with salt and pepper to taste.

SUPER SIMPLE PEANUT SOUP

One pantry ingredient I cannot be without is peanut butter. In a moment of creative energy, I developed the following soup using two common vegetables, carrots and broccoli, with Asian Peanut Sauce and some chicken stock.

Makes 4 cups (1 L), about 3 servings

2 cups	chicken or vegetable stock	500 mL
I cup	Asian Peanut Sauce (see recipe, page 122) or store-bought	250 mL
2 cups	small broccoli florets	500 mL
I cup	thinly sliced carrots	250 mL
	Salt and freshly ground black pepper	

1. In a medium saucepan over high heat, bring chicken stock, peanut sauce, broccoli and carrots to a boil. Reduce heat. Cover and cook slowly, stirring occasionally, for 10 minutes or until vegetables are tender.

2. Season with salt and pepper to taste.

TOMATO BASIL SOUP

This very quick version of the classic tomato soup is just right for a refreshingly light supper. Serve it hot in winter with toasted French bread and cheese (see Serving Suggestion, below) or cold in summer. Look to the fresh tomato variation below for even more flavor when tomatoes are in season.

Makes 6 cups (1.5 L), about 5 servings

Fresh Tomato Basil Variation
Replace canned tomatoes with 6 large peeled and diced tomatoes. Add ¼ cup (50 mL) tomato paste during the cooking and follow method using all ingredients.

3 cups	chicken stock	750 mL
3	cloves garlic, minced	3
1	can (28 oz/798 mL) diced tomatoes	1
1 cup	fresh basil leaves, thinly sliced	250 mL
	Salt and freshly ground black pepper	

1. In a large saucepan over high heat, bring stock, garlic and tomatoes to a boil. Reduce heat. Cover and cook slowly for 20 minutes.

2. Remove from heat. Cool slightly before puréeing half of soup in a food processor or blender until smooth. Repeat with remaining soup.

3. Return to saucepan. Add basil and reheat to serving temperature. Season with salt and pepper to taste.

SERVING SUGGESTION

- Toasted French bread spread with light Boursin cheese is a great stand-in for the more traditional toasted cheese sandwich. Lightly spread each slice of crusty bread with cheese. Place on broiler pan. Broil for 2 minutes or until lightly browned and cheese is melted.

SEAFOOD CHOWDER

This chowder is perfect for two people at lunchtime, suppertime or any other time.

Makes 3 cups (750 mL), about 2 servings		

I	can (7.5 oz/213 g) salmon, undrained		I
I	can (5 oz/142 g) whole baby clams, undrained		I
I	medium potato, peeled and diced (see Tip, left)		I
I cup	light (5%) cream or evaporated milk		250 mL
	Salt and freshly ground black pepper		

TIP
If you have a leftover cooked potato, just dice and delete potato cooking in Step 2. Continue with recipe.

1. Remove skin from salmon and discard. Flake salmon into coarse pieces.

2. In a medium saucepan over high heat, bring salmon, clams and potato to a boil. Reduce heat, cover and cook slowly, stirring occasionally, for 10 minutes or until potato is tender.

3. Add cream and reheat slowly to serving temperature. Season with salt and pepper to taste.

MOROCCAN LENTIL SOUP

This lentil-and-chickpea soup is a wonderful addition to vegetarian recipes. You can replace the vegetable stock with beef or chicken stock for non-vegetarians.

Makes 6 cups (1.5 L), about 5 servings		

I	large onion, chopped		I
	Special Seasonings, optional (see Seasoning Tip, page 33)		
I cup	red lentils		250 mL
4 cups	vegetable stock		I L
I	can (19 oz/540 mL) chickpeas, drained and rinsed		I
	Salt and freshly ground black pepper		

recipe continues on page 33

Red Pepper Aioli *(page 13)* ▶

SEASONING TIP
Turmeric, paprika, cumin and cayenne pepper are frequently added to this soup to provide a more authentic North African flavor. Add the spices to the onions while they soften. At serving time, garnish with chopped cilantro for color.

1. In a large saucepan over medium heat, sauté onion with a little water or oil until softened. Stir in Special Seasonings (see Tip, left), if using. Add lentils and stock.

2. Bring to a boil over high heat. Reduce heat, cover and cook slowly, stirring occasionally, for 30 minutes or until lentils are soft.

3. Stir in chickpeas. Season with salt and pepper to taste.

SPANISH GARLIC SOUP

This soup is reminiscent of the classic French onion soup, but because the stock is clear, it is lighter. The garlic flavor is distinct, but not harsh. Accompany the soup with sliced toasted crusty bread and grated Parmesan cheese.

Makes 6 cups (1.5 L), about 5 servings

10	cloves garlic, peeled and sliced	10
3 tbsp	olive oil	45 mL
5 cups	beef stock	1.25 L
1 cup	dry sherry	250 mL
	Salt and freshly ground black pepper	

1. In a large saucepan over medium heat, sauté garlic in oil for 1 minute or until golden (but not browned).

2. Add stock and sherry. Bring to a boil. Reduce heat, cover and cook slowly for 30 minutes. Season with salt and pepper to taste. Strain garlic and discard.

SERVING SUGGESTION
• Place toasted slice of crusty bread in the bowl and pour soup over it. Sprinkle lightly with Parmesan and serve.

AVGOLEMONO SOUP

Avgo (eggs) and lemono (lemon) are the basis for this light Greek specialty. It appears on menus all over Greece. After you have combined all the ingredients, cook on low heat to prevent the eggs from curdling. Some chopped fresh parsley adds eye appeal.

<table>
<tr><td>Makes 5 cups (1.25 L), about 4 servings</td><td>4 cups</td><td>strong chicken stock (see Tip, left)</td><td>1 L</td></tr>
<tr><td></td><td>1 cup</td><td>cooked rice</td><td>250 mL</td></tr>
<tr><td></td><td>4</td><td>eggs</td><td>4</td></tr>
<tr><td></td><td>2</td><td>lemons</td><td>2</td></tr>
<tr><td></td><td colspan="2">Salt and freshly ground black pepper</td><td></td></tr>
</table>

TIP
Simmer a homemade or good-quality stock for 30 to 45 minutes to concentrate flavor.

1. In a medium saucepan over high heat, bring stock and rice to a boil.

2. In a small bowl, beat eggs until frothy. Squeeze juice from 1 lemon (about ¼ cup/50 mL) and beat in. Gradually whisk in about ½ cup (125 mL) hot stock, beating constantly.

3. Reduce heat to low. Return mixture to saucepan with remaining soup. Whisk until soup is thickened. Season with salt and pepper to taste. Thinly slice remaining lemon and garnish each serving with a lemon slice.

STRAWBERRY SOUP FRAPPÉ

When the weather is hot and sticky, this soup is ideal for a summer meal. Make it in large amounts and freeze some for later use.

<table>
<tr><td>Makes 4 cups (1 L), about 3 servings</td><td>3 cups</td><td>halved strawberries</td><td>750 mL</td></tr>
<tr><td></td><td>1 cup</td><td>unsweetened pineapple juice</td><td>250 mL</td></tr>
<tr><td></td><td>2 tbsp</td><td>granulated sugar</td><td>25 mL</td></tr>
<tr><td></td><td>1 cup</td><td>plain yogurt</td><td>250 mL</td></tr>
<tr><td></td><td colspan="2">Mint leaves, optional</td><td></td></tr>
</table>

SEASONING TIP
Some additional seasonings to consider are lemon juice and grated zest, which are always tasty in fruit soup. Ground cinnamon or nutmeg provide a neat flavor hit.

1. In a food processor or blender, purée strawberries, pineapple juice and sugar until smooth.

2. Transfer to a covered container. Whisk in yogurt. Cover and freeze for about 3 hours or until it reaches a slushy consistency.

3. Serve scoops in chilled soup dishes, garnished with a mint leaf, if using.

CHILLED CUCUMBER SOUP

Flavors really improve when this refreshing soup is made a day ahead. The recipe makes more than you may want but it can be easily halved. It keeps refrigerated for several days. It was adapted from an Ontario Greenhouse Growers booklet.

Makes 6 cups (1.5 L), about 5 servings

2	English cucumbers, peeled and coarsely chopped	2
2 cups	plain yogurt or light sour cream	500 mL
2 tbsp	chopped fresh dill	25 mL
I tsp	freshly squeezed lemon juice	5 mL
6	ice cubes	6
	Salt and white pepper	

1. In a food processor or blender, purée cucumber, yogurt, dill, lemon juice and ice cubes until very smooth.

2. Transfer to a covered container. Refrigerate for 2 hours or until well chilled. Season with salt and pepper to taste.

WATERMELON GAZPACHO SOUP

Shirley Ann and Alan served this soup to us one hot summer day.
They could hardly contain themselves as we tried to guess
the ingredients. We never did. Why not try this on your guests as well?
Hard to believe the unknown ingredient is watermelon!

**Makes 6 cups
(1.5 L), about
5 servings**

TIP
This soup freezes
very well. It is
worth making in
large quantity in the
summer. This way,
you can serve it
at a time when
watermelon is
pricey or not
readily available.

5 cups	cubed watermelon	1.25 L
4	slices day-old white bread	4
⅔ cup	ground almonds	150 mL
1	clove garlic	1
10	ice cubes	10
	Salt and freshly ground black pepper	
	Chopped chives, optional	

1. In a food processor or blender, purée watermelon in batches until very smooth. Set aside.

2. Remove crusts from bread. Tear bread into small pieces. Add bread, almonds, garlic and ice cubes to final batch of watermelon purée. Purée until very smooth. Combine with remaining puréed watermelon.

3. Season with salt and pepper to taste.

BREAKFASTS, BRUNCHES & BREADS

FOR YEARS, MOTHERS HAVE SAID THAT BREAKFAST (AND THIS CAN INCLUDE brunch) is the most important meal of the day. And for good reason. This is the meal that starts off your day and fuels your brain and muscles. It's the first nourishment taken after the nightly fast. Skipping it puts you at a disadvantage that generally lasts all day.

The good things that make breakfast and brunch such a treat are all in this chapter: cereals, eggs, quick breads and pancakes, all the old-fashioned comfort foods to delight the dedicated breakfast eater.

The word "brunch" was first coined around 1900, for the meal that is too early to be a main meal, yet too late to be breakfast. But the term has come to mean much more. There is an air of comfortable civility and leisurely satisfaction evoked by an invitation to brunch. Unlike the potentially intimidating cocktail party or sophisticated "dinner at eight" invitation, somehow casual enjoyment is guaranteed at this late-morning event. The recipes in this chapter fit both brunch and breakfast equally well.

HUEVOS RANCHEROS

The Spanish word for eggs is huevos. This recipe for the all-time favorite Mexican breakfast is lower in fat than its namesake down south. Warm flour tortillas and serve with the huevos.

Serves 4		
1	can (14 oz/398 mL) black beans, drained and rinsed	1
1 cup	mild or medium salsa	250 mL
4	eggs	4
½ cup	shredded Cheddar or Monterey Jack cheese	125 mL

1. In a skillet, over medium heat, combine beans, salsa and ¼ cup (50 mL) water. Heat to boiling, stirring often.
2. Crack eggs onto surface of bubbling mixture. Reduce heat to low, cover, and cook for 5 minutes or until eggs are set.
3. Sprinkle with cheese and serve.

MUSHROOM EGG SCRAMBLE

This quick egg dish makes breakfast a special event for mushroom lovers. Earthy mushroom flavors combine with the taste of fresh eggs for an elegant breakfast experience. Serve over whole wheat toast or toasted English muffin halves.

Serves 1 to 2		
1 tbsp	butter or margarine	15 mL
2	large button mushrooms, sliced	2
2	eggs	2
2 tbsp	milk	25 mL
	Salt and freshly ground black pepper	

1. In a nonstick skillet over high heat, melt butter. Add mushrooms and cook, stirring often, for 5 minutes or until golden brown.

2. Whisk together eggs, milk, salt and pepper. Reduce heat to low. Pour egg mixture into skillet with mushrooms, stirring occasionally until eggs are set.

CHEESE-BAKED EGGS

This is the easiest and the very best way to cook eggs without watching them! Serve with a slice of fresh melon and whole wheat toast. Our young grandson Will loves them. He calls them "Nanna's eggs."

Serves 4 to 6

Cheese Variations
Any of the hard cheeses that shred well may replace Swiss. Use Cheddar or Monterey Jack for Mexican-style, Asiago or Provolone when you want to go Italian or small dollops of chèvre cheese for a French influence.

• PREHEAT OVEN TO 350°F (180°C)
• 8-INCH (2 L) BAKING PAN, GREASED

¾ cup	shredded Swiss cheese	175 mL
6	eggs	6
⅔ cup	milk or light (5%) cream	150 mL
	Salt and freshly ground black pepper	
	Finely chopped fresh parsley or basil, optional	

1. Sprinkle cheese over bottom of prepared pan. Break eggs over cheese.

2. Whisk together milk and salt and pepper to taste. Pour over eggs.

3. Bake in a preheated oven for 15 minutes or until eggs are just set. Sprinkle with chopped parsley, if using.

HOT CEREAL
WITH MULTIGRAINS

*Sometimes known as "the mighty oat," rolled oats and other whole grains
are such nutritional powerhouses that the U.S. Department of Agriculture urges
you to use them for half of the suggested six daily servings of grain-based products.
Furthermore, rolled oats impart a nutty tang to cereals that is positively addictive.*

Makes 3 cups (750 mL)

TIPS

Ingredients such as wheat flakes can be found in bulk or health food stores. Rye flakes or cracked wheat are good replacements for wheat flakes.

To release the health benefits of flaxseed, the hard outer coating must be broken down. You can buy flax meal or easily prepare your own. This is best done using a blender, a mini food processor or a coffee grinder.

DRY CEREAL MIX

2 cups	large flake rolled oats	500 mL
$\frac{1}{2}$ cup	wheat flakes (see Tips, left)	125 mL
$\frac{1}{2}$ cup	oat bran	125 mL
$\frac{1}{4}$ cup	flaxseeds, divided	50 mL

1. In a medium bowl, combine rolled oats, wheat flakes and oat bran.

2. Place half of flaxseeds in a small blender or coffee grinder (see Tips, left). Process to fine meal. Combine flaxseed meal and remaining seeds with rolled oat mixture. Store in a tightly sealed container for several weeks or for longer storage in the refrigerator.

FOR SINGLE SERVING

Microwave

1. In a microwave-safe serving bowl, combine $\frac{1}{4}$ cup (50 mL) Dry Cereal Mix, $\frac{3}{4}$ cup (175 mL) water and dash vanilla or maple extract. Microwave, uncovered, on High for 2 minutes. Stir. Microwave on Low for 3 minutes. Let stand for 2 minutes. Stir and serve.

Stove-top

1. In a small saucepan, over medium heat, bring $\frac{1}{4}$ cup (50 mL) Dry Cereal Mix, $\frac{3}{4}$ cup (175 mL) water and dash vanilla or maple extract to a boil. Reduce heat to low. Cook, stirring occasionally, for 3 minutes or until desired consistency. Cover and remove from heat. Let stand for a few minutes. Stir and serve.

SERVING SUGGESTION
• Dried fruit such as apricots, raisins, cherries and cranberries are all excellent additions.

CINNAMON RAISIN FRENCH TOAST

French toast, that agreeable combination of egg and bread, is a hit with all ages. It can be made the night before, allowing faster serving to your gang on busy mornings.

Makes 8 slices

Maple Variation
Follow Step 1 but add ¼ cup (50 mL) maple syrup for a delicate flavor addition.

• *NONSTICK COOKING SPRAY*

3	eggs	3
⅓ cup	milk	75 mL
1 tsp	ground cinnamon	5 mL
8	slices raisin bread	8

1. In a shallow dish, whisk together eggs, milk and cinnamon.

2. Dip each bread slice into egg mixture. Turn to coat, soaking up egg mixture.

3. Spray a large nonstick skillet with cooking spray. Add bread slices, in batches as appropriate. Cook over medium heat for 2 minutes. Turn and cook for 2 minutes more or until golden brown. Serve warm.

OVEN-BAKED VERSION

1. Place bread in a lightly greased shallow baking pan large enough for 8 slices. Pour egg mixture over bread. Bake in 425°F (220°C) oven for 18 minutes or until bread is toasted and golden.

SERVING SUGGESTION
- Maple syrup or fresh fruits such as strawberries, raspberries, peaches or bananas are ideal with these crispy toasts.

PUFFY OVEN PANCAKES

On our annual spring getaway to Niagara-on-the-Lake, we were served this awesome pancake. Anita, our B & B hostess, brought it piping hot from the oven at the peak of perfection. She suggested serving it with poached sliced apples or, of course, with maple syrup.

Serves 2		

TIP
This recipe is easily doubled to serve more people.

- *PREHEAT OVEN TO 425°F (220°C)*
- *NONSTICK COOKING SPRAY*
- *TWO SMALL OVAL BAKING PANS OR CUSTARD CUPS*

½ cup	all-purpose flour	125 mL
½ cup	milk	125 mL
2	eggs	2
I tsp	vanilla extract	5 mL

1. In a small bowl, whisk together flour, milk, eggs and vanilla (mixture will be lumpy).

2. Heat baking pans in oven for 5 minutes or until they are hot. Spray with cooking spray.

3. Divide batter between dishes. Bake in preheated oven for 15 minutes or until puffy and golden. Turn oven off, keeping pancakes inside for 5 minutes or until set.

4. Remove pancakes to warm serving plates and serve at once.

SOUR CHERRY CREAM CHEESE SPREAD

Dried sour cherries are now quite readily available; however, if you are unable to find them, dried cranberries work just fine. This spread is absolute perfection on a toasted bagel.

Makes ½ cup (125 mL)		

½	package (8 oz/250 g) cream cheese, softened	½
2 tbsp	chopped dried sour cherries	25 mL
2 tbsp	chopped toasted almonds	25 mL
I tsp	liquid honey	5 mL

1. In a small bowl, stir together cheese, cherries, almonds and honey until smooth.

2. Spoon into a covered container. Store in the refrigerator for up to 3 weeks until ready to use.

EGG SALAD SPREAD

I use this spread for a sandwich filling, sometimes at brunch or even at breakfast. It is especially good as an appetizer for dipping raw vegetables by younger ones. And try it on a toasted bagel! It's a good spread to take on a picnic because no mayonnaise is used.

Makes 1 cup (250 mL)

TIP
A pastry blender is also an easy way to chop eggs.

4	hard-cooked eggs	4
¼ cup	plain yogurt or sour cream	50 mL
I tsp	Dijon mustard	5 mL
2	green onions, chopped	2
	Salt and freshly ground black pepper	

1. Remove shells from eggs and discard.

2. In a food processor, chop eggs with on/off motion. Add yogurt, mustard, onions and salt and pepper to taste. Pulse briefly just until well mixed (see Tip, left).

3. Spoon into a covered container. Store in refrigerator for up to 2 days.

GRILLED VEGETABLE GOAT CHEESE SANDWICH

Inspired by a deli restaurant sandwich my husband raved about, and since I already had a recipe for grilling vegetables, this was a snap to develop. If you're short of time, grilled vegetables can be picked up at any deli counter. How can anything this easy taste so good?

Serves 1		
2	thick slices crusty Italian bread	2
2 tbsp	creamy goat cheese	25 mL
3	slices grilled eggplant (see Grilled Vegetables, page 146)	3
3	slices grilled green or red bell pepper (see Grilled Vegetables, page 146)	3
	Salt and freshly ground black pepper	

1. Place bread on a flat surface. Carefully spread one slice with cheese right out to the crust.

2. Arrange eggplant and pepper slices over cheese. Sprinkle lightly with salt and pepper.

3. Top with second slice of bread. Cut in half and serve.

ASPARAGUS MELT SANDWICH

Use either Basil Pesto Sauce or a commercial one for this recipe. Add crusty bread, steamed asparagus spears, sliced cheese, possibly a Provolone or mozzarella, and I guarantee this sandwich will be a major success.

Serves 2	• PREHEAT BROILER	
12	asparagus spears	12
2 tbsp	Basil Pesto Sauce (see recipe, page 132) or store-bought	25 mL
2	thick slices crusty Italian bread	2
2	slices Provolone or mozzarella cheese	2
	Freshly ground black pepper	

1. Snap tough ends from asparagus. Steam for 2 minutes or until tender-crisp. Then immerse in cold water to stop cooking. Drain and set aside on paper towels to dry.

2. Spread pesto evenly over each bread slice. Top each with 6 asparagus spears and 1 slice cheese. Sprinkle with pepper.

3. Broil for 3 minutes or until cheese melts. Serve warm.

POPOVERS

Popovers are such an easily made quick bread. Serve hot with jam and butter at snack time or for breakfast. But don't forget their most traditional use at dinner as Yorkshire pudding with roast beef cooked in the beef drippings.

Makes 6 large popovers

TIP
Since most of us own 12-cup muffin pans, add some water to remaining 6 cups without batter. This will help to prevent the pan from warping during baking.

• PREHEAT OVEN TO 425°F (220°C)
• 6-CUP MUFFIN PAN, GREASED AND FLOURED

I cup	all-purpose flour	250 mL
½ tsp	salt	2 mL
2	eggs	2
I cup	milk	250 mL

1. In a small bowl, stir together flour and salt. Set aside.

2. In another bowl, whisk together eggs and milk. Stir into flour mixture until blended but still lumpy. Spoon into prepared muffin cups, filling three-quarters full.

3. Bake in preheated oven for 15 minutes. Reduce heat to 350°F (180°C) and continue baking for 15 minutes or until puffed and browned.

4. Turn oven off, keeping popovers inside for 10 minutes to dry. Remove from pans, pierce sides of popovers with a toothpick for steam to escape. Serve immediately.

SODA BREAD

Soda bread is a quick bread that is leavened with baking soda in combination with an acid such as buttermilk. The best known one is Irish Soda Bread.

<table>
<tr><td>Makes 1 large loaf or two small</td></tr>
</table>

TIPS
You may find you will need extra buttermilk if the dough is too dry.

Currants or raisins may be added to make this soda bread into a sweeter one.

The same dough is used to make strawberry shortcake. Just add a pinch of granulated sugar to the dough.

• *PREHEAT OVEN TO 375°F (190°C)*
• *BAKING SHEET, GREASED*

4 cups	whole wheat flour	1 L
2 cups	all-purpose flour	500 mL
1 tsp	baking soda	5 mL
1 tsp	salt	5 mL
3 cups	buttermilk, approx. (see Tips, left)	750 mL

1. In a large bowl, combine whole wheat and all-purpose flours, baking soda and salt.

2. Pour enough buttermilk into dry ingredients to make a thick dough. Stir well. With floured hands, place dough on a lightly floured surface and flatten into a circle about $1\frac{1}{2}$ inches (4 cm) thick.

3. Transfer dough to prepared baking sheet. Make a cross on the top with a sharp knife. Bake in preheated oven for 40 minutes or until a cake tester inserted in center comes out clean.

4. Let cool on pan on a wire rack for 10 minutes. Transfer from pan onto rack to cool completely.

TUSCAN OLIVE BREAD

We rented a 400-year-old farmhouse for a month in Tuscany and the local baker kept us supplied with these fabulous hearty olive-filled breads.

<table>
<tr><td>Makes 1 loaf</td></tr>
</table>

• *BAKING SHEET, GREASED*

1 lb	loaf frozen white bread dough	500 g
$\frac{1}{2}$ cup	chopped pitted black kalamata olives	125 mL
$1\frac{1}{2}$ tsp	dried rosemary leaves	7 mL
1	egg white, lightly beaten	1
	Coarse salt	

1. Thaw dough or use dough prepared in your bread machine set on dough cycle.

2. On a floured board, sprinkle olives and rosemary over dough. Knead until they are incorporated into the dough. Cover and let rest for 10 minutes.

3. Roll dough with a floured rolling pin into a 10-by 8-inch (25 by 20 cm) rectangle. Place on prepared baking sheet, cover and set in a warm location to rise for 1 hour or until doubled in size.

4. Uncover and cut slits in top with a sharp knife. Brush with egg white and sprinkle with salt. Bake in 375°F (190°C) oven for 40 minutes or until loaf sounds hollow when tapped. Cool on a wire rack.

HOT CHEESE BREAD RING

This is an excellent quick bread snack. Or it can be an accompaniment to soup or salad. Add garlic powder or different herbs for a change in flavor.

Serves 8

• PREHEAT OVEN TO 375°F (190°C)
• 10-INCH (25 CM) TUBE PAN, GREASED

½ cup	shredded Cheddar cheese	125 mL
⅓ cup	light or regular mayonnaise	75 mL
½ tsp	dried oregano or 2 tsp (10 mL) chopped fresh	2 mL
1	package (10.5 oz/340 g) refrigerated country biscuits	1
	Chopped fresh parsley, optional	

1. In a small bowl, combine cheese, mayonnaise and oregano.

2. Remove biscuits from package. Roll each into a ball and roll in cheese mixture. Place biscuits in prepared pan, layering as needed. Sprinkle with parsley, if using.

3. Bake in preheated oven for 30 minutes or until puffed and golden brown. Turn onto a serving plate. Serve warm.

SICILIAN FOCACCIA BREAD

While in Sicily, I had the pleasure of taking in a short cooking class to learn the basics of making the famous focaccia bread of the Regusa area in the eastern part of the island. We then took several warm loaves back to the villa we were renting for a superb lunch enjoyed with a glass of Sicilian red wine and luscious sliced tomatoes.

| **Makes 1 loaf** | | |

Variations
Follow Steps 1 and 2, then choose one of the following fillings:

Christmas Focaccia
Stir together
¼ lb (125 g) cooked ground lamb, 2 tbsp (25 mL) chopped parsley, ½ tsp (2 mL) salt and ¼ tsp (1 mL) freshly ground pepper.

Vegetable Focaccia
Cook 1 cup (250 mL) diced eggplant with ½ cup (125 mL) chopped broccoli and 2 tbsp (25 mL) chopped onion until softened. Season with salt and freshly ground black pepper to taste. Cool before spreading over dough.

• BAKING SHEET, LINED WITH PARCHMENT PAPER

1½ lbs	loaf frozen white bread dough	750 g
½ cup	ricotta cheese	125 mL
2 tbsp	freshly grated Parmesan cheese	25 mL
1 tbsp	chopped fresh parsley	15 mL
	Salt and freshly ground black pepper	

1. Thaw dough or use dough prepared in your bread machine set on dough cycle.

2. On a floured board, roll dough with a floured rolling pin into either a 10-by 10-inch (25 by 25 cm) square or round. Set aside.

3. In a small bowl, stir together ricotta and Parmesan cheeses. Stir in parsley, salt and pepper. Spread bottom half of dough with spoonfuls of this mixture. Cover cheese by bringing top part of dough over, pressing to seal at edges forming the dough into a shape like a loaf of bread. Place on prepared pan. Cover and set in a warm location to rise for 1 hour or until doubled in size.

4. Uncover and cut slits in top with a sharp knife. Bake in 375°F (190°C) oven for 30 minutes or until loaf sounds hollow when tapped. Remove from oven to a rack to cool. Cut with a serrated bread knife into thick slices and serve.

SALADS & SALAD DRESSINGS

SALADS ARE NOT ONLY LOVELY TO LOOK AT BUT ARE AN IMPORTANT nutritional component of all our diets. And they are so versatile — serve them as a meal in themselves, as one course in a larger meal or as a side dish. According to Homer, salads were a favored food of the gods. So, a typical Greek meal was meat, bread, cheese and dessert followed by a crisp vegetable salad.

Salads are usually thought of as last-minute foods. In fact, molded and marinated salads should be made several hours ahead or the night before. For a quick make-ahead tossed salad, try this idea: place the dressing in the salad bowl. Add some chunky vegetables such as tomatoes, cucumber, carrots and celery. Only at the last minute top all of this with salad greens and toss. (For more information on making salads, see page 9.)

RASPBERRY VINEGAR

*The technique used in this recipe produces a more intense
fruit flavor than is found in many raspberry vinegars. As a result,
you can use it more sparingly. There is not the same botulism
potential with flavored vinegars as there is with flavored oils.
The acid level of vinegar prevents growth of the botulism organism.*

**Makes 2 cups
(500 mL)**

2 cups	raspberries, fresh or frozen and thawed	500 mL
1¼ cups	red or white wine vinegar	300 mL
⅓ cup	granulated sugar	75 mL

1. Place raspberries, vinegar, sugar and ¼ cup (50 mL) water in a medium stainless steel or enamel saucepan. Bring to a boil over high heat. Reduce heat. Cover and boil gently for 5 minutes. Let cool to room temperature. Cover and refrigerate overnight.

2. Next day, strain through a coffee filter or cheesecloth-lined sieve, pressing to extract liquid. Discard pulp. Pour liquid into a clean jar with a tight-fitting lid. Store in the refrigerator for up to one year.

BASIC FRESH HERB VINEGAR

*Fresh herb vinegars are so expensive to buy, yet are so very
easy to make. So why not make some in the summer while
fresh herbs are inexpensive and readily available?*

**Makes 2 cups
(500 mL)**

2 cups	vinegar (see Tips, above right)	500 mL
½ cup	fresh herbs, crushed (see Tips, above right)	125 mL

1. In a saucepan, bring vinegar to a boil.

Suggested Vinegars:
red wine, white
wine, cider, rice or
white vinegar.

Seasoning Tip: sage,
basil, thyme, dill,
tarragon, rosemary,
oregano or chives or
any combination
you like.

2. Place herbs in a clean jar. Add boiling vinegar. Cover
   and steep in a sunny location for 2 weeks or longer.

3. When vinegar has absorbed the herb flavor, strain
   vinegar through a coffee filter or cheesecloth-lined
   sieve into a second clean jar with a tight-fitting lid.
   Discard herbs. Add a fresh sprig of the herb, if
   desired. Store in the refrigerator for up to one year.

HOW TO DRY HERBS

- Put a single layer of herbs between three layers of paper
  towels. Microwave on High for 2 minutes or until herbs are
  dry. Store in a closed container in a cool dark place for up
  to six months.

JELLIED GAZPACHO

Here is the easiest jellied salad imaginable.
Thanks to Darlene, a busy friend, who gave me the recipe.

Serves 6 to 8

TIPS
To make unmolding
easier for any jellied
recipe, rinse the mold
with cold water.

If you don't want
to go to the trouble
of removing the
salad from the mold
at serving time,
refrigerate it in
an attractive 6-cup
(1.5 L) serving bowl.

• 6-CUP (1.5 L) MOLD

1	package (3 oz/85 g) lemon-flavored gelatin	1
1	can (19 oz/398 mL) Italian-style stewed tomatoes	1
1 cup	diced cucumber	250 mL
¼ cup	diced green bell pepper or sliced green onions	50 mL

1. In a small bowl, stir gelatin with 1 cup (250 mL)
   boiling water until gelatin is completely dissolved.

2. In a large bowl, combine tomatoes, cucumber and
   green pepper. Stir in gelatin.

3. Rinse mold with cold water (see Tip, left). Ladle in
   mixture. Cover and refrigerate for 2 hours or until set.

MUSHROOM ORANGE SALAD

*Refreshing and interesting, this salad goes well with many entrées.
Arrange a bed of mesclun on a serving platter or individual salad plates
and top with the mushroom-orange mixture at serving time.*

Serves 4		

3 tbsp	olive oil	45 mL
½ cup	rice vinegar	125 mL
2	oranges	2
1 lb	small button mushrooms	500 g
	Salt and freshly ground black pepper	

1. Place oil and vinegar in a small saucepan. Remove zest from oranges and add to saucepan. Bring to a boil on high heat. Reduce heat and cook for 3 minutes. Remove from heat. Add mushrooms. Set aside.

2. When cooled, transfer mushrooms and liquid to a bowl. Season with salt and pepper to taste.

3. Slice oranges and stir into mixture. Cover and refrigerate for about 6 hours before serving.

TIP

Mushroom Storage
Since mushrooms have a respiration rate, store them loosely in either a paper bag or under paper towels in the refrigerator to keep them moist. Do not store them wet. Use them within two to three days because they develop wrinkles and brown spots and spoil quickly.

MARINATED ASPARAGUS

*Marinating vegetables is much like a pickling process. Once they
are marinated, they keep refrigerated for several days.*

Serves 4		

1 lb	asparagus	500 g
1	clove garlic, minced	1
½ cup	rice vinegar	125 mL
2 tbsp	granulated sugar	25 mL
	Salt and freshly ground black pepper	

Variation
Carrots, green beans and broccoli florets are excellent marinated in the same method used for asparagus.

1. Snap off asparagus ends. Steam for 2 minutes or until tender-crisp. Immerse in cold water. Drain and set aside to dry. Place in a shallow container.

2. Combine garlic, vinegar, sugar, salt and pepper. Pour mixture over asparagus.

3. Cover and refrigerate for 1 hour. Remove asparagus from vinegar and serve at room temperature.

MARINATED MUSHROOMS

Mix and match any mushroom — portobello, button, shiitake, oyster — all can be marinated using this recipe.

Serves 4

TIP
Choose the freshest mushrooms — firm and evenly colored, not broken and with tightly closed caps. If the gills are showing, they are past their prime. To prepare, wipe with a damp paper towel or a mushroom brush.

2 cups	sliced mushrooms (see Tip, left)	500 mL
2 tbsp	white vinegar	25 mL
I tbsp	extra virgin olive oil	15 mL
2 tbsp	chopped fresh parsley	25 mL
	Salt and freshly ground black pepper	

1. Place mushrooms in a shallow container.

2. In a small bowl, whisk together vinegar, oil, parsley, salt and pepper. Pour over mushrooms. Let stand at room temperature for several hours before serving. Drain before serving.

THE "FAMOUS" BEAN SALAD

This salad uses either bottled red wine vinaigrette or one of the homemade ones found in this chapter. Sometimes, I add a can of drained chickpeas as a replacement for one of the beans.

<table>
<tr><td rowspan="2">Serves 4</td><td>2 cups</td><td>beans, a mix of green and yellow, cooked or canned</td><td>500 mL</td></tr>
<tr><td>1 cup</td><td>canned kidney beans, drained and rinsed</td><td>250 mL</td></tr>
<tr><td>TIP
Kept refrigerated, this salad lasts for several days.</td><td>½ cup</td><td>chopped red onion</td><td>125 mL</td></tr>
<tr><td></td><td></td><td>Salt and freshly ground black pepper</td><td></td></tr>
<tr><td></td><td>¼ cup</td><td>red wine vinaigrette or Sun-Dried Tomato Vinaigrette or Tomato French Dressing (see recipes, page 64)</td><td>50 mL</td></tr>
</table>

1. In a medium bowl, combine all beans with onion. Sprinkle lightly with salt and pepper.

2. Pour vinaigrette over vegetables and refrigerate for several hours before serving.

MINTED GREEN SALAD

An excellent refreshing salad to complement lamb,
chicken and with certain pastas.

Serves 6		
6 cups	mixed greens	1.5 L
¼ cup	coarsely chopped mint	50 mL
2 tbsp	extra virgin olive oil	25 mL
	Juice and zest of 1 lemon	
	Salt and freshly ground black pepper	

TIP
If the flavor is too sharp, a pinch of granulated sugar softens the tartness of any dressing.

1. In a large salad bowl, combine mixed greens and mint.
2. In a small bowl, whisk together oil, lemon juice and zest, salt and pepper. Toss dressing with greens at serving time.

MINTED FRUIT SALAD

Combine fresh seasonal fruits with refreshing mint leaves to make this
dynamite salad. I always prefer using one berry, then add other fruits
as they are available. Serve over leafy lettuce for sumptuous eye appeal.

Serves 4		
¼ cup	orange juice	50 mL
2 tbsp	liquid honey	25 mL
1 cup	diced mango or honeydew or cantaloupe balls	250 mL
	Fresh chopped mint leaves	

Berry Variations
Strawberries, blueberries, raspberries, blackberries or Saskatoon berries, all offer a pleasant addition to this melon salad.

1. In a medium bowl, whisk together juice and honey. Add mango. Sprinkle with a small amount of chopped mint.
2. Cover and refrigerate for 1 hour.

ASIAN RICE FRUIT SALAD

My family loves this salad with roast pork, lamb or cold ham and in the summer as a side salad to grilled chicken. Prepare the accompanying Asian Citrus Salad Dressing while cooking the rice. It is best to make the salad ahead so it can mellow with the dressing.

Makes 3 cups (750 mL)

Variation
Asian Rice Vegetable Salad
Sometimes I add frozen blanched peas instead of the grapes. Then I also use chopped red onions and omit the apricots.

1	package (6 oz/180 g) wild and white rice mix	1
½ cup	halved green seedless grapes	125 mL
¼ cup	diced dried apricots	50 mL
¼ cup	Asian Citrus Salad Dressing (see recipe, below) or store-bought oil and vinegar with an Asian flavor	50 mL
	Salt and freshly ground black pepper	

1. Cook rice mix according to package directions. (You will have about 2 cups/500 mL.) Allow to cool.

2. In a large bowl, combine rice, grapes and apricots.

3. Drizzle with ¼ cup (50 mL) dressing or more if you wish a stronger flavor. Taste and season with salt and pepper.

ASIAN CITRUS SALAD DRESSING

This dressing goes with the Asian Rice Fruit Salad (see recipe, above). It also adds wonderful flavor served over steamed fish.

Makes about ½ cup (125 mL)

1	orange	1
2 tbsp	sesame oil	25 mL
1 tbsp	soy sauce	15 mL
1 tbsp	rice vinegar	15 mL
	Salt and freshly ground black pepper	

If you want a stronger Asian flavor, add 1 large clove garlic minced and 1 tbsp (15 mL) minced fresh gingerroot.

1. Grate 1 tsp (5 mL) zest from orange and squeeze out juice to make ¼ cup (50 mL), reserve any extra for another use. Place zest and juice in a container with a tight fitting lid. Add oil, soy sauce and vinegar. Shake well to combine. Season with salt and pepper to taste.

2. Refrigerate for several days or up to one week.

ITALIAN PASTA INSALATA

Reflecting my love of things Italian, this has become a favorite basic pasta salad. It takes on many different looks and tastes, depending on what I add. You will no doubt have many additions based on your pantry supplies.

Serves 6

TIPS
Rotini can be replaced by any other pasta that is firm and has a shape to hold the marinade. Spaghetti-like pastas do not work.

You can also make additions such as diced red or green bell peppers, green onions, diced tomatoes or cooked vegetables such as frozen peas or mixed vegetables.

4 cups	cooked rotini pasta (see Tip, left)	1 L
½ cup	sliced black olives	125 mL
1	jar (6 oz/170 mL) marinated artichoke hearts	1
2 tbsp	balsamic or red wine vinegar	25 mL
	Salt and freshly ground black pepper	

1. In a large bowl, combine rotini and olives.

2. Drain artichokes reserving marinade. Chop and add artichokes to rotini.

3. Add vinegar to the reserved marinade. Toss with pasta mixture. Season lightly with salt and pepper.

CABBAGE AND CARROT SLAW

This traditional coleslaw is an especially great salad to make for a potluck — it travels well because it does not contain any mayonnaise.

Serves 4		
2 cups	thinly sliced cabbage	500 mL
1 cup	small carrot strips	250 mL
2 tbsp	cider vinegar	25 mL
1 tbsp	extra virgin olive oil	15 mL
	Salt and freshly ground black pepper	

1. In a salad bowl, combine cabbage and carrots.

2. Add vinegar and oil and toss to combine. Season lightly with salt and pepper. Cover and refrigerate for at least one hour before serving.

BROCCOLI MANDARIN SALAD

This salad can be described as a "meaty" one that everyone is bound to like (even if they never touch broccoli). Broccoli is available year-round but the homegrown is best when in season.

Serves 6		
1	head broccoli, trimmed and cut into small florets	1
½ cup	golden raisins	125 mL
1	can (10 oz/284 mL) mandarin oranges, drained	1
½ cup	bottled creamy garlic dressing (see Tip, left)	125 mL
	Salt and freshly ground black pepper	

TIP
There are many varieties of creamy garlic dressing available.
In this recipe, use either a commercial one or Creamy Curry Dressing (see recipe, page 62). I also add chopped red onion and toasted almonds or sunflower seeds for their nutty flavor.

1. In a large bowl, combine broccoli, raisins, oranges and dressing. Season lightly with salt and pepper.

2. Cover and refrigerate for several hours before serving.

THE PERFECT TOMATO SALAD

Its ingredients are traditional — black olives, feta cheese and olive oil — but this is definitely not your usual Greek salad. It is a delightful change!

Serves 6		

3	large tomatoes, halved	3
½ cup	crumbled feta cheese	125 mL
¼ cup	chopped black olives	50 mL
2 tbsp	extra virgin olive oil	25 mL
	Salt and freshly ground black pepper	

TIP

Feta is a young crumbly cheese. Originally it was made from goat's or sheep's milk but today is more commonly made from cow's milk. It is cured and stored in its own brine. Stored in brine in the refrigerator, it will remain fresh for about 2 weeks.

1. Scoop pulp from center of tomato halves. Reserve pulp. Place halves upside-down on paper towel to drain.

2. In a small bowl, combine half of tomato pulp, cheese, olives, oil, salt and pepper. Chill for 1 hour.

3. At serving time, spoon tomato mixture into tomato halves and serve. Use remaining pulp for Garlic Tomato Mayonnaise (below).

GARLIC TOMATO MAYONNAISE

This dressing is ideal to serve over The Perfect Tomato Salad (see recipe, above) or over sliced tomatoes.

Makes about ½ cup (125 mL)		

¼ cup	tomato pulp (about 1 tomato)	50 mL
¼ cup	mayonnaise	50 mL
2 tbsp	chopped fresh parsley	25 mL
1	clove garlic, minced	1

TIP

To peel tomatoes, cut a shallow "x" in the end opposite the stem and immerse tomato in boiling water for 10 seconds. Transfer to ice water. Tomato peels easily.

1. Stir tomato pulp with mayonnaise, chopped fresh parsley and garlic. A spoonful of this dressing makes a tasty topping for a tomato salad.

LEMON-DILL
WHITE BEAN SALAD

Bean salads are always useful because they can be made ahead.
Fresh dill and lemon make this one zesty and fresh tasting.

Serves 4		

TIP
Try this with red kidney beans instead of white and a green pepper instead of red or a mix of all.

I	can (19 oz/540 mL) white kidney beans, drained and rinsed (see Tip, left)	I
¼ cup	chopped red onion	50 mL
¼ cup	diced red bell pepper	50 mL
2 to 3 tbsp	Lemon Vinaigrette (see recipe, below) or store-bought	25 to 45 mL
	Freshly ground black pepper	

1. In a medium bowl, stir together beans, onion and red pepper.
2. Add dressing and pepper to taste. Cover and refrigerate for several hours or overnight.

LEMON
VINAIGRETTE

This very useful vinaigrette is one to keep on hand in the refrigerator.
Enjoy it with cooked vegetables such as asparagus, green beans
or broccoli or drizzled over fish fillets before baking or grilling.

Makes ½ cup (125 mL)		

⅓ cup	extra virgin olive oil	75 mL
3 tbsp	freshly squeezed lemon juice	45 mL
2 tbsp	chopped fresh dill	25 mL
	Salt and freshly ground black pepper	

1. In a container with a tight-fitting lid, combine oil, lemon juice and dill. Cover and shake well to blend. Season with salt and pepper to taste.

2. Store in the refrigerator for up to 2 weeks.

SERVING SUGGESTION

Asparagus Salad

- Arrange blanched asparagus spears in a shallow dish. Drizzle with a small amount of Lemon Vinaigrette. Scatter with shaved Parmesan cheese and serve.

GINGERED APPLE SLAW

A change from the usual cabbage slaw, this fresh-tasting salad capitalizes on the affinity of apples and ginger. It is excellent with pork or ham.

Serves 4		
½ cup	light mayonnaise	125 mL
1 tbsp	rice or cider vinegar	15 mL
1 to 2 tsp	finely chopped fresh gingerroot	5 to 10 mL
4	apples, peeled, cored and cut into julienne strips	4
	Salt and freshly ground black pepper	

1. In a medium bowl, whisk together mayonnaise, vinegar and gingerroot to taste.

2. Stir in apples. Toss to combine. Season lightly with salt and pepper.

CREAMY TOFU HERB DRESSING

This excellent fresh-tasting high-protein dressing goes well on either a green salad or coleslaw. Or use it as a dip!

Makes 1½ cups (375 mL)		

1 cup	buttermilk	250 mL
4 oz	silken tofu, drained (approx. ½ cup/125 mL chopped)	125 g
2 tbsp	chopped fresh dill	25 mL
1 tbsp	chopped fresh oregano or 1 tsp (5 mL) dried	15 mL
	Salt and freshly ground black pepper	

TIP
Tofu is excellent used in stir-fries, salads, casseroles and sandwiches. It is easy to digest, low in calories and sodium, high in protein and cholesterol-free. The more whey is removed, the firmer the tofu.

1. In a food processor or blender, blend buttermilk and tofu until smooth. Transfer to a container with a tight-fighting lid. Stir in dill, oregano, salt and pepper.

2. Cover and refrigerate for up to one week.

CREAMY CURRY DRESSING

This versatile salad dressing is great with a cabbage coleslaw or try it as a dip with sliced apples.

Makes ¾ cup (175 mL)		

½ cup	light mayonnaise	125 mL
¼ cup	plain yogurt	50 mL
1 tbsp	finely chopped fresh parsley	15 mL
1 to 2 tsp	curry powder	5 to 10 mL

1. In a small bowl, whisk together mayonnaise, yogurt, parsley and curry powder to taste.

2. Transfer to a covered container and refrigerate until chilled. The dressing keeps refrigerated for up to 5 days.

LAYERED SALAD

Since we all like recipes that can be made ahead, this attractive and tasty salad will become a favorite — a good start to any entertaining occasion.

Serves 6		

4 cups	shredded iceberg lettuce	I L
3	chopped green onions	3
I	can (19 oz/540 mL) kidney beans, drained and rinsed	I
⅓ cup	Sun-Dried Tomato Vinaigrette (see recipe, page 64) or store-bought equivalent	75 mL

TIPS

One of the creamy salad dressings such as the Creamy Curry Dressing (see recipe, page 62) is an interesting substitute for the vinaigrettes. Spoon it over the salad before refrigerating.

For extra protein, add a shredded cheese layer.

1. In a large serving bowl, arrange a layer of lettuce, topped by onions, then beans. Cover and refrigerate for several hours or overnight.

2. Just before serving, drizzle with Sun-Dried Tomato Vinaigrette or Tomato French Dressing, both on page 64. Toss and serve.

BASIL-FLAVORED OIL

Oil infused with fresh herbs has extraordinary flavor, yet is so simple to make. Serve it in a small bowl with a sprinkling of chopped fresh herbs and small pieces of crusty French bread for dipping.

Makes 1 cup (250 mL)		

• *PREHEAT OVEN TO 300°F (150°C)*

I cup	canola or extra virgin olive oil	250 mL
32	fresh basil leaves	32

Variation

Lemon and Dill
Add 2 tbsp (25 mL) lemon rind and 10 sprigs fresh dill to 1 cup (250 mL) oil. Heat for 1 hour and 40 minutes.

1. Place oil and basil in a 2-cup (500 mL) glass measuring cup. Set container on a pie plate. Bake for 1 hour and 40 minutes or until the herb is blackened and crisp. Let cool in dish on a rack for 30 minutes.

2. Line a small strainer with a coffee filter or several layers of cheesecloth. Strain oil into a clean glass jar. Discard leaves. Cover and store in the refrigerator at all times. Use oil within one month.

SUN-DRIED TOMATO VINAIGRETTE

Try to keep some of this vinaigrette in the refrigerator to use on the green salad you serve with pasta. The sun-dried tomatoes make this vinaigrette the perfect match. It is also used in the Layered Salad (see recipe, page 63).

	Makes ½ cup (125 mL)	

TIP
Liquid drained from sun-dried tomatoes can be added to soups and sauces.

½ cup	dry-packed sun-dried tomatoes (about 10)	125 mL
¼ cup	extra virgin olive oil	50 mL
2 tbsp	red wine vinegar	25 mL
1	clove garlic, minced	1
	Salt and freshly ground black pepper	

1. In a small bowl, pour boiling water over tomatoes. Let stand for 20 minutes or until softened. Drain, discard liquid and chop tomatoes into small pieces (see Tip, left).

2. In a container with a tight-fitting lid, combine tomatoes, oil, vinegar and garlic. Season with salt and pepper to taste. Cover and shake well to blend. Store in the refrigerator for up to 2 weeks.

TOMATO FRENCH DRESSING

An old favorite with a new twist — tomato vegetable cocktail is the magic ingredient that makes a wonderful French dressing with just four ingredients. When I use this dressing on a salad served with pasta, I cannot resist adding some grated Parmesan cheese.

	Makes 1¼ cups (300 mL)	

¾ cup	tomato vegetable cocktail	175 mL
⅓ cup	olive oil	75 mL
¼ cup	red wine or balsamic vinegar	50 mL
½ tsp	dry mustard	2 mL
	Freshly ground black pepper	

recipe continues on page 65

Cabbage and Carrot Slaw *(page 58)* ▶
Overleaf: Indian Chicken Kebabs *(page 83)*

1. In a container with a tight-fitting lid, combine vegetable cocktail, oil, vinegar and mustard. Cover and shake well to blend. Season with pepper to taste.

2. Store tightly covered, in the refrigerator for up to 2 weeks.

MAPLE DIJON SALAD DRESSING

The excellent maple-mustard flavors of this dressing go well with salads of greens and fruit. Refrigerate the dressing for a short time to allow flavors to mellow.

Makes ⅔ cup (150 mL)			
¼ cup	freshly squeezed lemon juice		50 mL
¼ cup	olive oil		50 mL
3 tbsp	maple syrup		45 mL
1 to 2 tsp	Dijon mustard		5 to 10 mL
	Salt and freshly ground black pepper		

1. In a container with a tight-fitting lid, combine lemon juice, oil, maple syrup and mustard to taste. Cover and shake well to blend.

2. Season with salt and pepper to taste. Store, tightly covered, in the refrigerator for up to 2 weeks.

SERVING SUGGESTION

- Trimmed fresh watercress, sliced fennel and sectioned oranges make an ideal combination dressed with these maple-mustard flavors.

TAPENADE VINAIGRETTE

*The robust black olive and balsamic flavors of this vinaigrette
are perfect added to a fresh green salad, making it
the ideal accompaniment to ham or beef.*

**Makes 1 cup
(250 mL)**

TIP
A standard-quality
balsamic is just fine
for this vinaigrette
because of the strong
tapenade flavors. A
better quality more
expensive balsamic
would be wasted.

½ cup	extra virgin olive oil	125 mL
3 tbsp	balsamic vinegar (see Tip, left)	45 mL
2 to 3 tbsp	Tapenade (see recipe, page 17) or store-bought	25 to 45 mL
2 tbsp	finely chopped fresh parsley or green onion	25 mL
	Salt and freshly ground black pepper	

1. In a container with a tight-fitting lid, combine oil, vinegar, tapenade to taste and parsley. Cover and shake well to blend. Season lightly with salt and pepper.

2. Store, tightly covered, in the refrigerator for up to 2 weeks.

TAPENADE MAYONNAISE

*Tapenade added to a light mayonnaise makes a really superb topping
for small new boiled potatoes or as a dip for crackers or raw vegetables.*

**Makes ½ cup
(125 mL)**

TIP
Replace mayonnaise
with plain yogurt for
a lighter-tasting
version with, of
course, less fat.

½ cup	light mayonnaise (see Tip, left)	125 mL
1 tbsp	balsamic vinegar	15 mL
1 tbsp	Tapenade (see recipe, page 17) or store-bought	15 mL
1 tbsp	finely chopped green onions	15 mL
	Freshly ground black pepper	

1. In a small bowl, whisk together mayonnaise, vinegar, tapenade and onions.

2. Season with pepper. Store, tightly covered, in the refrigerator for up to 2 weeks.

FISH & SEAFOOD

FISH PROVIDES A HANDSOME, VARIED AND DELICIOUS CHANGE OF PACE for your table. Whether salt or freshwater, frozen, canned or fresh, whole or cut, shellfish or fish without shell, fish should be part of your weekly diet. Thanks to modern shipping and freezing methods, fish is available to almost everyone regardless of geography.

Fish is a nutritious and low-fat protein alternative to meat. Its omega-3 fatty acids help fish play a role in reducing blood cholesterol levels. The fatter the fish, the greater the role. Omega-3 fatty acids help reduce the "stickiness" of blood platelets in arteries which in turn reduces risk of heart attack and stroke. Thus, fish rates highly as a heart-healthy food.

I often hear the comment, "When I cook fish, it is always dry." Overcooking is the primary cause of fish becoming dry during cooking. When overcooked, the proteins shrink, squeezing out the water, making fish both tough and dry. Fish cooks quickly because it is already tender and is held together by small amounts of connective tissue that dissolves easily when heated.

As a general guideline to cooking fish, Canada's Department of Fisheries recommends cooking it at a high temperature for 10 minutes per inch (2.5 cm) of thickness. Double cooking time if fish is frozen. This does vary somewhat depending on what cooking method is being used. Today there is a tendency for people to cook salmon to a medium-rare rather than well-done stage. Take 2 minutes off the cooking time for this less well-done stage. (For more information on fish and seafood, see page 6.)

When it comes to good nutrition, seafood is a natural choice!

BAKED MAPLE SALMON

Maple syrup adds an absolutely fabulous flavor to either salmon steaks or fillets. Another time, you might also like to try this with boneless chicken breasts.

Serves 6 to 8

FISH TIP
Salmon is a very healthy, nutritious food. Besides being an excellent source of protein and iron, salmon also contains more of the highly touted omega-3 fatty acids than most other fish.

- *PREHEAT OVEN TO 450°F (230°C)*
- *SHALLOW OBLONG PAN, GREASED*

1	large salmon fillet (about 2 to 3 lbs/1 to 1.5 kg)	1
½ cup	dry white wine	125 mL
2 tbsp	pure maple syrup or apple juice	25 mL
	Salt and freshly ground black pepper	
	Chopped fresh parsley	

1. Place fish skin-side down in prepared pan. Drizzle with wine and syrup. Season lightly with salt and pepper.
2. Bake for 10 minutes per inch (2.5 cm) of thickness or until fish is opaque and flakes easily when tested with a fork. Sprinkle with parsley and serve.

HERB-ROASTED SALMON

Salmon has such a marvelous flavor that little else is needed in the way of seasoning. This simple herb-oil mixture makes it easy. Mushroom Baked Rice (see recipe, page 126) is a good accompaniment to this recipe.

Serves 6

- *PREHEAT OVEN TO 450°F (230°C)*
- *SHALLOW OBLONG PAN, GREASED*

1	large salmon fillet (about 2 lbs/1 kg)	1
1 tbsp	olive oil	15 mL
2 tbsp	chopped fresh chives	25 mL
1 tbsp	chopped fresh tarragon or 1 tsp (5 mL) dried	15 mL
	Salt and freshly ground black pepper	

Whole salmon is best kept in the coldest part of the refrigerator at a temperature of less than 40°F (4°C), lightly covered with a damp towel. Store steaks, fillets and portions wrapped individually in sealed plastic bags, covered with ice.

1. Place fish skin-side down in prepared pan.

2. In a small bowl, combine oil, chives and tarragon. Rub half into flesh of salmon.

3. Bake for 10 minutes per inch (2.5 cm) of thickness or until fish is opaque and flakes easily when tested with a fork.

4. To serve, cut salmon in half crosswise. Lift flesh from skin with a spatula. Transfer to a platter. Discard skin, and then drizzle fish with remaining herbs and oil. Season lightly with salt and pepper.

SALMON WITH SPINACH

Salmon will remain moist using this cooking procedure. Layer spinach and mushrooms, then top with salmon. Bake on high heat for the recommended 10 minutes per inch (2.5 cm) thickness of the fish. Due to the extra thickness of fish and vegetables, you may need a few extra minutes of baking time.

Serves 4

Variations
As well as salmon, any white or firm-fleshed fish will do. These are turbot, swordfish, halibut or tuna. For ease of serving fish fillets, cut them into serving-size pieces before baking.

Crusty Layered Salmon
Sprinkle toasted sesame seeds over the fish before baking to give it a crusty crunch.

- PREHEAT OVEN TO 450°F (230°C)
- SHALLOW OBLONG PAN, GREASED

1	package (10 oz/300 g) frozen chopped spinach, thawed	1
1 tbsp	grated gingerroot	15 mL
2	large white mushrooms, thickly sliced	2
	Salt and freshly ground black pepper	
4	salmon steaks or fillets (see Variations, left)	4

1. In a sieve, drain spinach, pressing with a spoon to remove excess liquid. Discard liquid. Spread spinach in bottom of prepared pan in a shape resembling the size of the fish. Arrange gingerroot and mushrooms evenly over spinach. Season lightly with salt and pepper. Add fish. Sprinkle lightly with salt and pepper.

2. Cover pan loosely with a tent of foil. Bake for 15 minutes or until fish is opaque and flakes easily when tested with a fork.

STEAMED FISH FILLETS ASIAN-STYLE

This recipe is inspired by the Asian method of steaming fish on top of vegetables. Flavors will be fresher, colors richer and with only a small amount of fat.

Serves 4		

TIP
It's easier to skin a fillet than you may think. Place fillet, skin-side down, on a cutting board. Hold the tail end and firmly with one hand, cut skin away from flesh with quick, short strokes in a sawing motion. Slant knife blade at a 45-degree angle toward the skin so that no flesh is wasted.

1	small fennel bulb, trimmed and cut in half lengthwise	1
2	carrots, peeled and thinly sliced	2
1 lb	skinless salmon fillet (see Tip, left)	500 g
¼ cup	Asian Citrus Salad Dressing (see recipe, page 56) or store-bought oil and vinegar with an Asian flavor	50 mL
	Salt and freshly ground black pepper	

1. In a large nonstick skillet, place fennel and carrots. Add ¼ cup (50 mL) water.

2. Trim fish to fit pan, if necessary. Place in a single layer on top of vegetables. Drizzle with salad dressing. Season lightly with salt and pepper.

3. Cover and cook over medium-high heat for 12 minutes or until fish is opaque and flakes easily when tested with a fork.

GINGER-LIME FISH FILLETS

Any firm fish, such as swordfish, salmon, halibut or whitefish, will do for this recipe.

Serves 4		

• PREHEAT BROILER
• BROILER PAN, LIGHTLY GREASED

2	limes	2
2 tbsp	grated fresh gingerroot	25 mL
2 tbsp	liquid honey	25 mL
	Salt and freshly ground black pepper	
4	fish fillets (about ¾ inch/2 cm thick)	4

1. Grate 1 tsp (5 mL) zest from lime and squeeze out ½ cup (125 mL) juice, reserving any extra for another use. Place zest and juice in a shallow dish. Whisk in gingerroot, honey and salt and pepper to taste.

2. Dip fish into lime mixture. Place on prepared broiling pan. Broil for 10 minutes or until fish is opaque and flakes easily when tested with a fork.

3. Meanwhile, in a small saucepan over medium heat, bring remaining lime mixture to a boil. Cook until reduced by half. Drizzle warm sauce over fish and serve.

YOGURT-LIME FISH FILLETS

Take any fish fillet, such as salmon, whitefish, sole or turbot, add this easy sauce, and you will quickly have an elegant dinner for guests. Couscous with Vegetables (see recipe, page 124) is excellent to serve with the fish.

Serves 4

- *PREHEAT OVEN TO 450°F (230°C)*
- *SHALLOW OBLONG PAN, GREASED*

1 ¼ lbs	fish fillets	625 g
1	lime	1
¼ cup	plain yogurt	50 mL
1 tsp	ground cumin	5 mL
	Salt and freshly ground black pepper	

1. Place fish in prepared baking pan.

2. Grate ½ tsp (2 mL) zest from lime and squeeze out 2 tbsp (25 mL) juice, reserving extra for another use. Place zest and juice in a small bowl. Stir in yogurt, cumin and salt and pepper. Spoon over fish.

3. Bake for 10 minutes per inch (2.5 cm) of thickness or until fish is opaque and flakes easily when tested with a fork.

STEAMED FISH
WITH COUSCOUS

This fish dish is cooked in parchment. It makes easy work of both the serving and the cleanup.

Serves 4

TIP
Remember the rule of not overcooking fish. Since the packets are left to stand for 5 minutes, fish continues to cook enclosed in the foil or parchment.

- NONSTICK COOKING SPRAY
- PREHEAT OVEN TO 450°F (230°C)

I	onion, thinly sliced	I
I cup	couscous	250 mL
¾ cup	tomato juice	175 mL
4	sole or haddock fillets	4
	Salt and freshly ground black pepper	

1. Cut four pieces of parchment paper or foil 4 inches (10 cm) larger than fish fillets. Lightly spray with cooking spray. Divide onion equally on the four pieces of parchment. Add ¼ cup (50 mL) couscous to each.

2. Combine tomato juice with ½ cup (125 mL) water and a small amount of salt and pepper. Pour evenly over each portion of couscous. Top with fish.

3. Fold long ends of paper or foil twice so mixture is tightly enclosed. Lift short ends, bring together on top and fold twice. Place seam-side up on a baking pan.

4. Bake for 20 minutes or until fish flakes easily when tested with a fork and onion is tender. Remove from oven and let stand for 5 minutes or until couscous has absorbed all liquid. Open each package and serve contents on dinner plates.

> **MENU SUGGESTION**
> - A green vegetable, such as peas, green beans or sautéed zucchini, is a good accompaniment.

CUMIN-CRUSTED HALIBUT STEAKS

Sea bass, halibut, grouper or any dense whitefish are all excellent cooked in this interesting crust. It is preferable to use toasted cumin seeds as they have more flavor than ground cumin.

• PREHEAT OVEN TO 450°F (230°C)

Serves 4

1 tbsp	cumin seeds	15 mL
½ tsp	salt	2 mL
¼ tsp	freshly ground black pepper	1 mL
1 lb	halibut or other fish steaks	500 g
2 tsp	olive oil	10 mL
	Chopped fresh parsley, optional	

1. In a nonstick skillet over medium heat, toast cumin seeds, stirring, for 2 minutes or until golden. Place seeds, salt and pepper in a coffee or spice grinder. Pulse until finely ground. Rub mixture into both sides of fish.

2. Heat olive oil in a large nonstick skillet over medium-high heat. Add fish, in batches, if necessary, and cook for 2 minutes per side or until browned.

3. Return all fish to skillet and wrap handle with foil. Bake in preheated oven for 5 minutes or until fish is opaque and flakes easily when tested with a fork. Sprinkle with parsley, if using, and serve.

MENU SUGGESTION

- Broccoli and Red Onion Pasta (see recipe, page 125) and lemon wedges complete the plate.

BAKED FISH AND VEGETABLES EN PAPILLOTE

The term "en papillote" refers to steam baking in parchment paper or foil.
It's a fast, easy and healthy way to cook fish with vegetables.

<table>
<tr><td colspan="3">• NONSTICK COOKING SPRAY</td></tr>
<tr><td colspan="3">• PREHEAT OVEN TO 450°F (230°C)</td></tr>
<tr><td>4</td><td>fish fillets (each about ¼ lb/125 g)</td><td>4</td></tr>
<tr><td>4</td><td>large white mushrooms, sliced</td><td>4</td></tr>
<tr><td>2</td><td>green onions, sliced</td><td>2</td></tr>
<tr><td>20</td><td>snow peas, trimmed</td><td>20</td></tr>
<tr><td></td><td>Salt and freshly ground black pepper</td><td></td></tr>
</table>

Serves 4

TIP
Sliced carrots, zucchini, summer squash and sweet red or green bell peppers are all good choices to cook this way.

1. Cut four pieces of parchment paper or foil 4 inches (10 cm) larger than fish fillets. Lightly spray with cooking spray. Place each fillet in center of paper. Top each with 1 sliced mushroom, half the onions and 5 snow peas. Season lightly with salt and pepper.

2. Fold long ends of paper or foil twice so mixture is tightly enclosed. Lift short ends, bring together on top and fold twice. Place seam-side up on baking pan.

3. Bake for 20 minutes or until fish is opaque and flakes easily when tested with a fork and vegetables are tender. Open each package and serve contents on dinner plates.

POACHED JUMBO SHRIMP

I like to serve shrimp with Fresh Mango Salsa as a dipping sauce.
A green salad and cooked basmati rice complete the menu.

Serves 6		

½ cup	dry white wine	125 mL
2	sprigs fresh parsley	2
2	shallots, sliced	2
36	jumbo shrimp	36

1. In a large saucepan, bring wine, ½ cup (125 mL) water, parsley and shallots to a boil. Add shrimp. Reduce heat to medium and cook slowly for 4 minutes or until shrimp turn pink.

2. Remove with a slotted spoon to a bowl. Serve 6 shrimp per person with Fresh Mango Salsa (see recipe, below).

FRESH MANGO SALSA

Grilled or baked fish truly benefit when served with mango salsa.
I also like the sauce with shrimp or grilled chicken breasts.
For extra heat, add some finely chopped jalapeño pepper.

Makes 2 cups (500 mL)		

TIP

To check a mango's ripeness, hold it in your hand — it should feel like a good handshake, firm with a little give. To ripen further, store unripe mangoes at room temperature for 2 to 4 days in a paper bag, then store them in the refrigerator.

1	large ripe mango, peeled and finely diced (see Tip, left)	1
2	green onions, sliced	2
1 tbsp	extra virgin olive oil	15 mL
2 tsp	freshly squeezed lemon juice	10 mL
	Salt and freshly ground black pepper	

1. In a small bowl, stir together mango, onions, oil, lemon juice and salt and pepper to taste.

2. Cover and refrigerate for up to 2 days.

BASIL AND TOMATO FILLETS

Tomato and basil are natural partners. Add fish for a fresh delicious meal.

Serves 4			
2 tbsp	olive oil, divided	25 mL
1 lb	whitefish, tuna or salmon	500 g
	Salt and freshly ground black pepper	
½ cup	chopped firm tomatoes	125 mL
2 tbsp	chopped fresh basil leaves	25 mL

1. In a nonstick skillet over medium-high heat, heat 1 tbsp (15 mL) oil. Season fish lightly with salt and pepper. Add to skillet.

2. Combine tomatoes, basil and remaining oil. Top fish with spoonfuls of the mixture. Cover skillet tightly and cook on medium-high heat for 10 minutes or until fish is opaque and flakes easily when tested with a fork.

SERVING SUGGESTION

- My family enjoys Creamy Polenta (see recipe, page 130) with this fish recipe.

SEAFOOD QUESADILLAS

When you fill flour tortillas with a cheese, meat or fish mixture and then fold it over, it is called a quesadilla. The filling can include cooked or canned fish, meats, vegetables or refried beans. This easy shrimp filling is absolutely delicious!

Serves 4			
8	medium flour tortillas	8
½ cup	shredded Monterey Jack cheese	125 mL
1	can (4 oz/113 g) salad shrimp, drained and mashed (see Variations, left)	1
¼ cup	salsa, mild, medium or hot	50 mL

Variations
Any canned seafood, such as salmon, tuna, lobster or crabmeat, can replace the shrimp.

1. Place 4 tortillas on a flat surface.

2. In a bowl, combine cheese, shrimp and salsa. Divide mixture equally over each tortilla, spreading to the edge. Top with remaining 4 tortillas. Press edges gently to seal.

3. Heat a nonstick skillet over medium-high heat. One at a time, cook tortillas, turn once until browned and cheese is melted. Remove from pan. Continue with remaining tortillas. Using a pizza cutter or a sharp knife, cut each tortilla into quarters and serve.

OYSTER STEW

You either love oysters or hate them. For lovers, start a family tradition of serving this stew in December during the festive season. Shucked oysters simplify the stew's preparation. Good crusty bread is a must for enjoying all the juices.

Serves 4

TIPS
Shucked oysters spoil easily. Keep immersed in their liquid, tightly covered and refrigerated. They should keep for about one week.

Since oysters are low in calories, an excellent source of protein, iron and zinc, they make light eating at an otherwise heavy eating holiday season.

2½ cups	shucked oysters, undrained (see Tips, left)	625 mL
½ cup	finely chopped onion	125 mL
½ cup	finely chopped celery	125 mL
1	can (14 oz/385 mL) evaporated milk	1
	Salt and freshly ground black pepper	

1. If large, cut oysters into quarters. Strain liquid through a fine mesh sieve.

2. In a large saucepan, combine oysters, liquid, 1 cup (250 mL) water, onion and celery. Bring to a boil. Reduce heat to low. Cover and cook slowly for 5 minutes. Do not overcook, as oysters become tough. As soon as the edges curl, they are done.

3. Add milk and reheat to serving temperature. Season with salt and pepper to taste. Serve immediately.

STEAMED MUSSELS
WITH LIME

When buying mussels, make sure they are tightly closed.
If they are gaping open, lightly tap the shell to see if they will close.
Discard any that do not close.

Serves 4		

TIP
Storing Mussels
Keep mussels
covered with
a damp cloth in
a leak-proof
container, stored
in the coldest part
of the refrigerator
for several days.

36	mussels (see Tip, left)	36
2	limes	2
1 cup	dry white wine	250 mL
1 tbsp	granulated sugar	15 mL

1. Rinse mussels well under cold running water. Drain and set aside.

2. Grate zest and squeeze juice from both limes. Set aside.

3. In a large saucepan, bring wine, half the grated lime zest and sugar to a boil. Add mussels. Steam on high for 6 minutes or until they are open. With a slotted spoon, transfer mussels to a serving dish and keep warm.

4. Add remaining lime zest and reserved lime juice to mussel liquid. Gently boil until liquid is reduced by half. Pour over mussels and serve immediately.

SERVING SUGGESTION
- Crusty Italian bread is absolutely essential with mussels for soaking up their juices.

POULTRY

POULTRY IS AN ECONOMICAL, VERSATILE AND NATURALLY LEAN FOOD, making it a good protein choice. It includes a wide choice of feathered and winged fowl, but chicken is the most popular and most frequently served. Chicken is a delicate suggestible meat, ready to absorb flavor from wine, herbs, yogurt and sour cream, juices, bouillon, fruits and most vegetables. Hence, most of the recipes in this chapter are for chicken.

However, turkey is not forgotten. I well remember when turkey was once reserved for Christmas and Thanksgiving. When I was young, my grandfather always ordered a second turkey at Christmas for my early January birthday dinner. Happily, today it is readily available and economical throughout the year. For poultry tips, see page 7.

CHICKEN MOROCCAN-STYLE

Make Moroccan Marinade to have handy for this delicious chicken dish. Immerse the chicken in it for a marvelous African flavor. Try it with pork tenderloin for another African experience.

Serves 4		

TIPS

I much prefer marinating messy ingredients in a clean plastic bag. It is easier to turn the bag to coat the meat. You don't have to use a new bag — even a clean plastic milk bag will do.

The chicken may be grilled on a preheated barbecue with lid closed, if you prefer, rather than using the oven. Grill for about 8 minutes per side or until meat is no longer pink inside.

• BAKING SHEET, GREASED

4	skinless, boneless chicken breasts	4
	Moroccan Marinade (see recipe, page 81)	
²⁄₃ cup	dried bread crumbs	150 mL
½ tsp	ground cumin	2 mL

1. Trim fat from chicken and discard. Rinse and wipe with paper towel. Place chicken in a shallow dish. Pour marinade mixture over, turning to coat. Cover and refrigerate for at least 4 hours, turning chicken occasionally.

2. Place bread crumbs and cumin in a plastic bag (see Tip, left). Remove chicken from marinade. Discard marinade. Add chicken to crumbs, tossing to coat. Transfer to prepared baking sheet.

3. Preheat oven to 400°F (200°C). Bake chicken for 20 minutes or until meat is no longer pink inside (see Tip, left).

MENU SUGGESTION

- Rice Pilaf with Toasted Almonds (see recipe, page 127) and a salad complete the meal.

MOROCCAN MARINADE

This combination of everyday ingredients creates a marinade that gives an African touch to mild-flavored meats such as chicken or pork.

Makes ⅔ cup (150 mL)		
½ cup	plain yogurt	125 mL
1 tsp	grated orange zest	5 mL
2 tbsp	freshly squeezed orange juice	25 mL
2	cloves garlic, minced	2
	Salt and freshly ground black pepper	

TIP
To be more authentic, add a pinch of ground cinnamon.

1. In a small container, whisk together yogurt, orange zest and juice, garlic and salt and pepper.

2. Cover and refrigerate for up to 3 days to use as a marinade for chicken or pork.

APRICOT-GLAZED CHICKEN

Apricot and Dijon mustard add flavor interest to bland chicken legs.

Serves 6

• *PREHEAT OVEN TO 425°F (220°C)*
• *BAKING PAN, LIGHTLY GREASED*

6	chicken legs (about 2 lbs/1 kg)	6
⅓ cup	apricot jam	75 mL
1 to 2 tbsp	minced gingerroot or 1 tsp (5 mL) ground ginger	15 to 25 mL
1 tbsp	Dijon mustard	15 mL
	Salt and freshly ground black pepper	

1. Rinse and wipe chicken with paper towel and place on prepared baking sheet.

2. In a small bowl, combine jam, gingerroot, mustard and salt and pepper. Brush chicken with jam mixture.

3. Bake in preheated oven for 30 minutes or until meat is no longer pink inside.

CHICKEN WITH TOMATO MUSHROOM SAUCE

Here is another great use for Basic Red Tomato Sauce. Some cooked pasta,
such as a penne, makes a perfect accompaniment to the chicken.
With a green salad, you've got a complete meal.

Serves 2		
2	chicken legs	2
2 tsp	vegetable oil	10 mL
1 cup	Basic Red Tomato Sauce, mushroom variation (see recipe, page 120) or store-bought	250 mL
1 tsp	dried basil leaves or 1 tbsp (15 mL) chopped fresh	5 mL
	Salt and freshly ground black pepper	

1. Rinse and wipe chicken with paper towel and set aside.

2. Heat oil in a nonstick skillet over medium-high heat. Sauté chicken for 5 minutes or until brown.

3. Add sauce, basil, salt and pepper. Reduce heat. Cover and cook slowly for 30 minutes or until meat is no longer pink inside.

APPLE HARVEST CHICKEN

Everyone will enjoy this fast and tasty chicken recipe. Serve with
green beans and mashed potatoes for a simple weeknight dinner.

Serves 4	• NONSTICK COOKING SPRAY	
	4	skinless, boneless chicken breasts	4
	$\frac{1}{2}$ tsp	dried thyme leaves	2 mL
		Salt and freshly ground black pepper	
	2	medium apples, peeled and thickly sliced	2
	$\frac{1}{4}$ cup	apple cider or apple juice	50 mL

1. Rinse and wipe chicken with paper towel. Sprinkle with thyme, salt and pepper.

2. In a large nonstick skillet lightly sprayed with cooking spray, sauté chicken on medium-high for 5 minutes on each side or until browned.

3. Add apples and cider. Cover, reduce heat to medium-low and cook gently for 10 minutes or until meat is no longer pink inside.

INDIAN CHICKEN KEBABS

Curry and ginger provide a taste of India in this ever-so-easy-to-make entrée.

Serves 6	• SIX SKEWERS	
	6 skinless, boneless chicken breasts	6
	½ cup low-fat plain yogurt	125 mL
	1 tbsp grated gingerroot	15 mL
	1 tbsp curry paste	15 mL
	Salt and freshly ground black pepper	

1. Rinse and wipe chicken with paper towel. Cut into bite-size cubes.

2. In a bowl, whisk together yogurt, gingerroot, curry paste, salt and pepper. Add chicken and toss to coat. Cover and refrigerate for 1 hour.

3. Lightly grease barbecue and preheat to medium-high. Thread chicken loosely onto six skewers, discarding marinade. Place on prepared grill. Close lid and cook for 20 minutes, turning once or until meat is no longer pink inside.

MENU SUGGESTION

- Couscous with Vegetables (see recipe, page 124) and a green salad complete the menu.

MUSHROOM CHICKEN STROGANOFF

Sour cream and mushrooms combined with sautéed chicken make a stroganoff reminiscent of Eastern Europe.

Serves 4		

• NONSTICK COOKING SPRAY

4 cups	thickly sliced mushrooms	I L
⅔ cup	sour cream	150 mL
2 tsp	all-purpose flour	10 mL
	Salt, freshly ground black pepper and paprika	
4	skinless, boneless chicken breasts	4

1. In a large nonstick skillet lightly sprayed with cooking spray, sauté mushrooms, turning often, on medium-high for 6 minutes or until golden brown. Remove and set aside.

2. In a small bowl, whisk together sour cream, flour, salt, pepper and paprika. Set aside.

3. Meanwhile, rinse and wipe chicken with paper towel. Spray same skillet again and sauté chicken on medium-high for 5 minutes or until browned on each side. Add mushrooms and sour cream mixture. Cover, reduce heat to medium-low and cook slowly for 10 minutes or until meat is no longer pink inside.

MENU SUGGESTION

• Cooked egg noodles along with some roasted vegetables make an appetizing meal.

STUFFED CHICKEN BREASTS

Plump chicken breasts stuffed with a sun-dried tomato, mushroom and bread crumb filling are really quite tempting. Any mushroom will do but a portobello or shiitake are especially flavorful.

Serves 6

TIP

Chicken breasts stuffed in this way are very attractive when sliced and make a nice presentation. It is essential that chicken or turkey be stuffed just before roasting.

- *PREHEAT OVEN TO 425°F (220°C)*
- *SMALL ROASTING PAN*

6	skinless, boneless chicken breasts	6
6	dry-packed sun-dried tomatoes	6
½ cup	chopped mushrooms	125 mL
½ cup	soft bread crumbs	125 mL
	Salt and freshly ground black pepper	

1. Rinse and wipe chicken with paper towel. Place on a flat surface. Beginning at center of thicker end of breast, insert a small sharp knife horizontally, stopping about 1-inch (2.5 cm) from opposite end. Open incision with fingers to create a pocket.

2. In a small bowl, soak tomatoes in boiling water for 10 minutes. When tomatoes are softened, drain well and chop.

3. Combine tomatoes, mushrooms, bread crumbs, salt and pepper. Divide the tomato mixture evenly and place into each chicken pocket. Secure pocket with toothpicks or small skewers. Be sure to remove them before serving.

4. Place chicken in roasting pan. Bake in preheated oven for 18 minutes or until meat is no longer pink inside. Remove from oven. Let stand for 5 minutes, then cut each breast in several slices and serve.

MENU SUGGESTION

- Served with a green salad and roasted vegetables baked at the same time as the chicken, makes this a fabulous dinner for family or guests.

HONEY GLAZE FOR CHICKEN

Treat chicken wings, breast or legs to this zippy honey-garlic glaze.
It can be used on chicken at the barbecue or in the oven to create
a glazed surface. Make extra for future dinners.

Makes ⅓ cup (75 mL)		

- PREHEAT OVEN TO 350°F (180°C)
- RIMMED BAKING SHEET, LINED WITH FOIL

¼ cup	liquid honey	50 mL
2	cloves garlic, minced	2
2 tbsp	soy sauce	25 mL
I tbsp	cider vinegar	15 mL
	Freshly ground black pepper	

1. In a small bowl, combine honey, garlic, soy sauce, vinegar and pepper.

2. When you are ready to bake chicken, brush mixture on chicken pieces and place in prepared baking pan. Bake chicken in preheated oven for 30 minutes or until meat is no longer pink inside.

MUSTARD-LIME CHICKEN

Brush this honey, Dijon mustard and lime juice mixture on
chicken during grilling. It really peps it up.

Serves 4		

- PREHEAT BARBECUE

2	limes, divided	2
¼ cup	Dijon mustard	50 mL
¼ cup	liquid honey	50 mL
4	skinless, boneless chicken breasts	4

TIP

Moist Chicken Breast
How do some restaurants serve such tender, moist chicken? They submerge the breast in buttermilk for 3 to 4 hours in the refrigerator before cooking.

1. Cut one lime into slices. Set aside. Grate zest and squeeze out juice from remaining lime. Place lime zest and juice in a small bowl. Whisk in mustard and honey.

2. Rinse and wipe chicken with paper towel. Cook chicken on medium-high on preheated grill for 7 minutes per side, brushing often with mustard mixture. Grill until meat is no longer pink inside.

3. Serve with any remaining sauce and lime slices.

CRANBERRY CHICKEN BREASTS WITH MUSHROOMS

This is a perfect recipe for easy entertaining. Dried cranberries, white wine and mushrooms provide a sublime taste.

Serves 4

TIP
If the remaining liquid is too thin, stir a small amount of cornstarch with cold water into the hot liquid. Cook and stir until mixture thickens. Serve over chicken.

• *NONSTICK COOKING SPRAY*

4	skinless, boneless chicken breasts	4
	Salt and freshly ground black pepper	
1 ½ cups	sliced mushrooms	375 mL
½ cup	dry white wine	125 mL
¼ cup	dried cranberries	50 mL

1. Rinse and wipe chicken with paper towel. Sprinkle lightly with salt and pepper.

2. In a large nonstick skillet lightly sprayed with cooking spray, sauté chicken on medium-high for 5 minutes on each side or until browned. Remove and set aside.

3. Add mushrooms to skillet. Cook for 5 minutes or until mushrooms are browned. Return chicken to skillet. Add wine and cranberries. Cover and cook on medium-low heat for 10 minutes or until meat is no longer pink inside. Serve with pan juices (see Tip, left).

SERVING SUGGESTION
• Serve with cooked fluffy rice to sop up any remaining pan juices.

CHICKEN BURRITOS

Wraps, as they are best known today, are really old-fashioned Mexican flour tortillas wrapped around a filling of your choice.

Serves 4		

TIP
Sour cream and extra salsa are great for toppings.

• PREHEAT OVEN TO 325°F (160°C)

4	flour tortillas (10 inch/25 cm)	4
2 cups	slivered cooked chicken or turkey	500 mL
¾ cup	salsa, mild, medium or hot	175 mL
½ cup	shredded Monterey Jack or Cheddar cheese	125 mL

1. Arrange tortillas on a flat surface. Place one-quarter each of chicken, salsa and cheese onto each wrap. Roll securely. Place seam-side down on baking pan.

2. Bake in preheated oven for 15 minutes or until cheese melts and wraps are warm.

MOZZARELLA TOMATO CHICKEN

This Italian-style treatment of chicken breasts keeps them so moist and flavorful that your family will call for it again and again.

Serves 4		

• PREHEAT OVEN TO 350°F (180°C)
• SHALLOW BAKING DISH, GREASED
• NONSTICK COOKING SPRAY

4	skinless, boneless chicken breasts	4
1	can (10 oz/284 mL) condensed tomato soup, undiluted	1
1 tsp	dried basil leaves or 1 tbsp (15 mL) chopped fresh	5 mL
½ cup	shredded mozzarella cheese	125 mL

1. Rinse and wipe chicken with paper towel. In a large nonstick skillet lightly sprayed with cooking spray, sauté chicken on medium-high heat for 5 minutes on each side or until browned.

2. Transfer chicken to prepared baking dish. Combine soup and basil. Spoon over chicken and sprinkle with cheese. Cover and bake in preheated oven for 20 minutes or until meat is no longer pink inside.

MEDITERRANEAN CHICKEN

My husband and I enjoyed this wonderful chicken entrée in a suburban bistro in London, Ontario. This is my version that uses both Basil Pesto Sauce and Tapenade.

Serves 4	

TIP
Chicken breasts vary in size, but the thicker the breast, the more you may need to pound to obtain an even thickness.

Pork Variation
Cut pork tenderloin lengthwise with a sharp knife until almost through to other side. Open meat and spoon tapenade-pesto filling down center. Fold meat over and tie with string. Bake at 375°F (190°C) for 30 minutes or until meat thermometer registers 170°F (80°C).

• PREHEAT OVEN TO 350°F (180°C)
• SHALLOW BAKING PAN

4	skinless, boneless chicken breasts	4
2 tbsp	Tapenade (see recipe, page 17) or store-bought	25 mL
1 tbsp	Basil Pesto Sauce (see recipe, page 132) or store-bought	15 mL
½ cup	dry white wine or chicken stock	125 mL
	Salt and freshly ground black pepper	

1. Rinse and wipe chicken with paper towel. Place chicken breasts on a flat surface. Pound with a mallet or the dull side of a large knife to flatten breasts to an even thickness (see Tip, left), about 1 inch (2.5 cm).

2. In a small bowl, stir together tapenade and pesto. Spoon equal amounts over two chicken breasts. Top with remaining two breasts. Secure edges with several toothpicks or tie with string.

3. Place chicken in baking pan. Add wine, salt and pepper. Cover with foil and bake in preheated oven for 20 minutes. Remove foil. Bake an additional 20 minutes or until meat is no longer pink inside. Slice each into 4 slices. Serve 2 slices per person.

CHICKEN AND PEACHES

Peaches give moisture and a delicate fruit flavor to chicken.
Turkey cutlets also work well in this recipe. Served with cooked
Asian noodles and steamed snow peas, this is a light and low-fat meal.

Serves 4		

SEASONING TIP
Adding ground
ginger or gingerroot
gives an extra
Asian flavor.

4	skinless, boneless chicken breasts	4
2 tsp	sesame oil	10 mL
2	large ripe peaches, peeled and sliced	2
3	green onions, cut into 1-inch (2.5 cm) pieces	3
	Salt and freshly ground black pepper	

1. Rinse and wipe chicken with paper towel. Set aside.

2. Heat oil in a large nonstick skillet on medium-high heat. Sauté chicken for 5 minutes on each side or until brown.

3. Add peaches and onions. Sprinkle lightly with salt and pepper. Cover and cook for 15 minutes or until meat is no longer pink inside. Serve chicken with juices and peach slices.

BAKED PARMESAN CHICKEN LEGS

My ongoing love for foods Italian is reflected in this recipe
for chicken pieces coated in Parmesan cheese and mustard.

Serves 8		

• *PREHEAT OVEN TO 425°F (220°C)*
• *RIMMED BAKING SHEET, LINED WITH PARCHMENT PAPER*

3 tbsp	Dijon mustard	45 mL
	Salt and freshly ground black pepper	
8	chicken legs (about 2½ lbs/1.25 kg)	8
2	English muffins	2
⅓ cup	freshly grated Parmesan cheese	75 mL

1. In a shallow bowl, whisk together mustard, 2 tbsp (25 mL) water and salt and pepper. Place chicken pieces in mixture, turning to coat well (see Tip, left).

2. Pulse muffins in a food processor until finely ground. Transfer crumbs to a plastic bag. Add cheese.

3. Remove chicken from mustard mixture, discarding remaining mixture. Toss chicken in crumbs, one piece at a time, until crumbs stick to chicken. Transfer to prepared baking sheet.

4. Bake in preheated oven for 30 minutes or until crumbs are golden brown and meat is no longer pink inside.

EAST INDIAN CHICKEN

In keeping with Indian tradition, plain yogurt, grated gingerroot, some cumin or curry are added to flavor chicken. Yogurt helps to keep the chicken moist during baking.

Serves 4

• PIE PLATE, LINED WITH FOIL

4	skinless, boneless chicken breasts	4
¾ cup	plain yogurt	175 mL
2 tsp	minced gingerroot	10 mL
I tsp	cumin (see Tip, left)	5 mL
	Salt and freshly ground black pepper	

1. Rinse and wipe chicken with paper towel. Place chicken in a resealable plastic bag.

2. In a glass measuring cup, stir together yogurt, gingerroot, cumin, salt and pepper. Pour over chicken in bag and seal. Refrigerate for several hours or overnight.

3. Preheat oven to 350°F (180°C). Transfer chicken to prepared pan. Bake for 20 minutes or until meat is no longer pink inside.

GRILLED CHICKEN WITH LEMON-HERB SAUCE

The chicken may be grilled on the barbecue or baked in the oven.
Immersing the cooked chicken in the lemon-herb sauce provides
an after-cooking marinated approach that is absolutely delicious.

Serves 6 to 8		
¼ cup	freshly squeezed lemon juice	50 mL
¼ cup	chopped fresh oregano leaves	50 mL
¼ cup	chopped fresh chives	50 mL
	Salt and freshly ground black pepper	
8	chicken pieces, such as breasts or drumsticks	8

1. Stir together lemon juice, oregano, chives and salt and pepper. Pour into a serving dish large enough to hold all chicken pieces.

2. Rinse and wipe chicken with paper towel. Grill at medium-high heat or roast until meat is no longer pink inside, about 20 minutes.

3. When chicken is cooked, transfer to bowl with lemon mixture. Turn to coat and serve.

SERVING SUGGESTION

- Serve lemon-herb coated chicken over assorted tossed greens with slices of fresh lemon, Caramelized Vidalia Onions (see recipe, page 161) and crusty rolls.

ROAST CHICKEN
WITH LEEKS

Whole chicken roasted with lemon and garlic has been a favorite of mine since I first tasted it in Italy. Fresh leeks roasted with the meat are simply marvelous.

Serves 6

TIP
You can use chicken stock or wine instead of water, if desired.

• PREHEAT OVEN TO 325°F (160°C)
• ROASTING PAN

I	roasting chicken (about 3 lbs/1.5 kg)	I
I	lemon, quartered	I
6	cloves garlic, sliced	6
2	large leeks, trimmed and washed	2
	Salt and freshly ground black pepper	

1. Rinse and wipe chicken with paper towel. Place breast-side down in a roasting pan. Stuff cavity with lemon and garlic.

2. Slice leeks in half lengthwise. Place cut-side down in roasting pan alongside chicken. Sprinkle with salt and pepper. Pour in ³⁄₄ cup (175 mL) water (see Tip, left). Cover tightly.

3. Roast in preheated oven for 40 minutes. Remove from oven and transfer leeks to a dish and keep warm. Return chicken to oven. Continue roasting, uncovered, for about 1½ hours or until meat thermometer registers 180°F (82°C). Remove chicken from oven. Let stand for 5 minutes before carving. Serve with leeks and any pan juices.

MENU SUGGESTION

• Crème Fraîche Mashed Potatoes (see recipe, page 147) are great for soaking up the wonderful pan juices. Carrots or asparagus in the spring when they are in season are always a joy.

TURKEY WILD RICE CRANBERRY STUFFING

Wild rice makes a wonderful and unique poultry dressing, especially for turkey. Make this stuffing the day before you need it and refrigerate until ready to roast your turkey. It is sufficient stuffing for a medium-size (10 to 12 lb/4.5 to 5.5 kg) turkey.

Makes 6 cups (1.5 L)			
1 ¼ cups	wild rice		300 mL
2 cups	chopped onion		500 mL
¼ cup	butter or margarine		50 mL
¾ cup	dried cranberries		175 mL
	Salt and freshly ground black pepper		

1. In a large saucepan over high heat, bring 5 cups (1.25 L) water and rice to a boil. Reduce heat to low, cover and cook for 40 minutes or until rice is tender. Remove from heat. Drain, if needed.

2. In a nonstick skillet, melt butter over medium heat. Add onion and cook, stirring, for 10 minutes or until tender. Stir into cooked rice. Add cranberries.

3. Let cool. Cover and refrigerate until chilled or overnight before using as stuffing.

TURKEY MEAT LOAF OLÉ

Meat loaf with a Mexican twist! Adding salsa provides extra flavor and moisture. Ground chicken may be used to replace turkey.

Serves 6		

• PREHEAT OVEN TO 375°F (190°C)
• 8-BY 4-INCH (1.5 L) LOAF PAN

2	eggs	2
¾ cup	salsa, mild, medium or hot, divided	175 mL
½ cup	dried bread crumbs	125 mL
1½ lbs	lean ground turkey or chicken	750 g

1. In a medium bowl, beat eggs with a fork. Stir in ¼ cup (50 mL) salsa, bread crumbs and ground turkey. Press into loaf pan. Spread remaining salsa over top.

2. Bake in preheated oven for 1¼ hours or until meat thermometer inserted in center registers 175°F (80°C). Let stand for 10 minutes. Drain off fat and cut into 6 slices.

HOW TO MAKE POULTRY STOCK

• Store poultry bones in the freezer until enough are accumulated to make a quantity of stock. Place these bones in a large saucepan. Add enough cold water to cover. Add chopped onion, chopped celery, sprigs of fresh parsley and bay leaves. Bring to a boil, cover and reduce heat. Simmer for about 2 hours. Allow to cool slightly at room temperature for 20 minutes. Pour liquid through a sieve into a pot. Discard vegetables and bones. Chill liquid and when cold remove any congealed fat and discard. Freeze to use when chicken or turkey stock is called for in recipe.

HERBED ROAST TURKEY ROLL

Turkey adapts readily to added flavorings, especially to herbs, spices and garlic. The finished roast carves into neat slices to enjoy hot or cold.

<table>
<tr><td>Serves 10</td><td colspan="3">• PREHEAT OVEN TO 325°F (160°C)</td></tr>
<tr><td></td><td>1</td><td>turkey roll (about 4 lbs/2 kg)</td><td>1</td></tr>
<tr><td></td><td>10</td><td>large cloves garlic, minced</td><td>10</td></tr>
<tr><td></td><td>3 tbsp</td><td>chopped fresh rosemary
or 1 tbsp (15 mL) dried</td><td>45 mL</td></tr>
<tr><td></td><td>1 tsp</td><td>salt</td><td>5 mL</td></tr>
<tr><td></td><td>¼ tsp</td><td>freshly ground black pepper</td><td>1 mL</td></tr>
<tr><td></td><td>2 tbsp</td><td>olive oil</td><td>25 mL</td></tr>
</table>

1. Place turkey roll on a cutting board and unroll as flat as possible.

2. In a small bowl, combine garlic, rosemary, salt, pepper and oil. Spread half of mixture over inside of turkey. Reroll and tie firmly with string. Spread remaining mixture over outside of roll.

3. Roast on a rack in preheated oven for 1½ hours or until a meat thermometer registers 180°F (82°C). Remove from oven and let stand for 10 minutes before carving.

Busy Day Stew *(page 102)* ▶

Overleaf: Marmalade-Glazed Pork Roast *(page 113)*

MEATS, SAUCES & MARINADES

THE SKILL OF COOKS IS GENERALLY JUDGED BY THE EXCELLENCE OF the meat course. So, it is important for anyone preparing meals to know the basic facts of buying and preparing a variety of meats, be it expensive steak cuts or pot roast (see page 8 for cooking and handling information).

As for marinades, they have probably been used as a cooking technique ever since people have been eating meat. It used to be that the main purpose of marinating was to tenderize tough wild game and to minimize the gamey flavor. Today, our hunting expeditions take us to the supermarket where we track down cuts of meat raised specifically for our tables. Today, we marinate to enhance the flavor and aroma of meat. Nevertheless, marinating can still turn a less expensive cut of meat into tender and delicious eating.

◄ Roasted Red Pepper Pasta Sauce *(page 120)*

SPECIAL MAKE-AHEAD BEEF MIXES

Busy people are always on the lookout for speedy ideas for food preparations. Following are three prepared mixes, which produce eight recipes between them — all perfect extra meals for the freezer.

Makes 4 dinners

Make this beef mix recipe ahead, divide in four, and you're ready to make four different dinners: Sloppy Joes and Beef Meat Loaf (see page 100) and Stuffed Green Peppers and Beef-Crust Pizza (see page 101).

BASIC TOMATO BEEF MIX

4 lbs	lean ground beef	2 kg
2	large onions, finely chopped	2
2	small green bell peppers, chopped	2
2	cans (each 28 oz/798 mL) diced tomatoes	2
	Salt and freshly ground black pepper	

1. In a large nonstick skillet or saucepan, cook beef over medium-high heat until brown and crumbly, stirring occasionally. Drain and discard fat. Return meat to pan, add onion and cook for 5 minutes more.

2. Add green peppers and tomatoes. Cover and simmer over medium-low, stirring occasionally, for 15 minutes or until mixture is cooked. Season with salt and pepper to taste.

3. Refrigerate to cool before dividing into four equal amounts. Refrigerate or freeze for future use.

Makes 2 stews

Make a large batch of this beef mixture and freeze for two fast dinners for later use. Then prepare either Busy Day Stew or Bavarian Stew (see page 102) and serve with hot crusty bread or rolls.

TWO-IN-ONE BEEF STEW MIXTURE

3 lbs	boneless cubed stewing beef, trimmed	1.5 kg
¼ cup	all-purpose flour	50 mL
2 tbsp	vegetable oil	25 mL
2	pouches (each 1.5 oz/45 g) dried onion soup mix	2

1. In a plastic bag, shake beef cubes with flour until meat is well coated.

2. In a large saucepan, heat oil on medium-high heat. Add meat, in batches, and sauté until browned. Return all meat with accumulated juices to pan.

Variation
Other liquids, such as beef stock, tomato juice, mushroom liquid or red wine, can be substituted for water.

**Makes
2 dinners**

Use this basic mixture for Beef 'n' Cheese Meat Loaf or Chili con Carne (see page 103). Or use half the mixture to shape into 4 patties or 12 meatballs. It's also excellent when you need a meat sauce for lasagna or pasta.

3. Combine soup mix and 2 cups (500 mL) water (see Variation, left). Pour over meat. Bring to a boil. Cover and reduce heat to medium-low and cook slowly for 40 minutes or until meat is almost tender.

4. Refrigerate to cool before dividing into two equal amounts. Refrigerate or freeze for future use.

BASIC BEEF MIXTURE

2 lbs	lean or medium ground beef	1 kg
1	large onion, chopped	1
2	cloves garlic, minced	2
1 cup	chopped mushrooms	250 mL
	Salt and freshly ground black pepper	

1. In a large nonstick skillet or saucepan over medium-high heat, brown beef, breaking into small chunks as it cooks. Brown for 8 minutes or until completely cooked. Drain fat and discard. Add onion, garlic and mushrooms. Cook for 5 minutes or until vegetables are cooked. Season with salt and pepper to taste.

2. Refrigerate to cool before dividing into two equal amounts. Refrigerate or freeze for future use.

SLOPPY JOES

*Kids and Sloppy Joes just go together. With Basic Tomato Beef Mix
prepared and waiting in your refrigerator or freezer, lunch for
school-age kids is on the table in less than 15 minutes.*

Serves 4		
¼	Basic Tomato Beef Mix (see recipe, page 98), thawed	¼
½ cup	chopped green pepper	125 mL
½ cup	chopped celery	125 mL
4	buns, split and toasted	4

1. In a saucepan, combine beef mixture with chopped green pepper and celery. Heat thoroughly for 10 minutes. Serve over toasted buns.

BEEF MEAT LOAF

*With the handy Basic Tomato Beef Mix in the refrigerator
or freezer, this meat loaf is a cinch to make.*

Serves 4	• PREHEAT OVEN TO 375°F (190°C) • 9-BY 5-INCH (2 L) LOAF PAN	
¼	Basic Tomato Beef Mix (see recipe, page 98), thawed	¼
½ cup	dry bread crumbs or rolled oats	125 mL
I	egg, beaten	I
I tsp	dried herbs (such as oregano, thyme or basil)	5 mL

1. Combine beef mix with dry bread crumbs, beaten egg and dried herbs. Mix well.

2. Spoon into loaf pan. Bake in preheated oven for 35 minutes or until firm. Let stand for 5 minutes before cutting into slices.

STUFFED GREEN PEPPERS

Stuffed green peppers are a classic. The Basic Tomato Beef Mix comes into play again in this scrumptious recipe.

Serves 6

• *PREHEAT OVEN TO 350°F (180°C)*

¼	Basic Tomato Beef Mix (see recipe, page 98), thawed	¼
1 cup	corn kernels	250 mL
1 tsp	Worcestershire sauce	5 mL
6	green bell peppers	6

1. Combine beef mixture with corn kernels and Worcestershire sauce. Mix well.

2. Remove tops of green peppers and seed. Parboil for 5 minutes in boiling water. Drain well.

3. Fill each pepper with one-sixth of mixture. Bake in preheated oven for 40 minutes or until tender.

BEEF-CRUST PIZZA

With Basic Tomato Beef Mix ready, this pizza is a snap to finish.

Serves 4

• *PREHEAT OVEN TO 400°F (200°C)*
• *9-INCH (23 CM) PIE PLATE*

¼	Basic Tomato Beef Mix (see recipe, page 98), thawed	¼
¼ cup	dry bread crumbs	50 mL
1 cup	sliced mushrooms	250 mL
½ cup	grated mozzarella cheese	125 mL

1. Combine beef mixture with dry bread crumbs. Mix well.

2. Press into pie plate. Top with sliced mushrooms and grated mozzarella cheese.

3. Bake in preheated oven for 20 minutes or until cheese is melted. Cut into wedges to serve.

BUSY DAY STEW

Since you have already partially prepared the beef mixture and frozen it, now finish the stew with the following recipe.

Serves 6		
1	package Two-in-One Beef Stew Mixture (see recipe, page 98), thawed	1
1	can (19 oz/540 mL) tomatoes	1
4	carrots, cut into chunks	4
1½ cups	peas, frozen	375 mL

Variation
Add caraway seeds to the stew while cooking for a great full flavor.

1. In a large saucepan, combine beef stew, tomatoes and carrots. Bring to a boil. Reduce heat. Cover and simmer for 25 minutes or until vegetables and meat are tender. Add peas during last 5 minutes of cooking. Extra liquid may be needed if mixture becomes too thick.

BAVARIAN STEW

Here's one more recipe using a package of the frozen beef stew.

Serves 6		
1	package Two-in-One Beef Stew Mixture (see recipe, page 98), thawed	1
2 cups	coarsely chopped cabbage	500 mL
1	can (10 oz/284 mL) mushrooms, including juice	1
1 cup	sour cream	250 mL

Variation
Other liquids, such as tomato juice or beef stock, can be substituted for water.

1. In a large saucepan, combine beef stew, 1 cup (250 mL) water, cabbage and mushrooms. Bring to a boil. Reduce heat. Cover and simmer for 10 minutes or until cabbage is tender-crisp.

2. Stir in sour cream and serve.

SERVING SUGGESTION
- Toss cooked egg noodles with caraway or poppy seeds. Top with Bavarian Stew and serve with crusty bread.

BEEF 'N' CHEESE MEAT LOAF

*In the wintertime, when so many activities take up much of
our free time, having a meat loaf to quickly pop in the oven
is a blessing. Basic Beef Mixture makes this possible.*

Serve 4

• *PREHEAT OVEN TO 375°F (190°C)*
• *9-BY 5-INCH (2 L) LOAF PAN*

½	cooked Basic Beef Mixture (see recipe, page 99), thawed	½
½ cup	shredded Cheddar cheese	125 mL
½ cup	rolled oats	125 mL
½ tsp	dried oregano leaves	2 mL

1. Combine cooked beef mixture with cheese, rolled oats and oregano.

2. Spoon into loaf pan. Bake in preheated oven for 35 minutes or until firm. Let stand for 5 minutes before slicing.

CHILI CON CARNE

*Basic Beef Mixture allows fast preparation of chili con carne.
Add a salad and dinner is on the table.*

Serves 4

½	cooked Basic Beef Mixture (see recipe, page 99), thawed	½
1	can (10 oz/284 mL) tomato soup	1
1	can (14 oz/398 mL) kidney beans, drained and rinsed	1
1 to 2 tsp	chili powder	5 to 10 mL

1. In a saucepan, combine cooked beef mixture, tomato soup, kidney beans and chili powder. Bring to a boil. Reduce heat, cover and simmer for 30 minutes or until mixture is thickened and ready to serve.

BEEF TENDERLOIN

This simple recipe is all it takes to make a gourmet treat of this succulent cut of beef. Using pork tenderloin is an equally tasty substitute.

Serves 4		

TIP
Beef suitable for this recipe is described as "grilling steak," indicating that the beef will be tender prepared in this fast cook grilling method. You can also use rib, rib eye, strip loin, T-bone and top sirloin.

1 lb	beef tenderloin (see Tip, left)	500 g
2 tsp	olive oil	10 mL
2	cloves garlic, sliced	2
1 tbsp	balsamic vinegar	15 mL
	Salt and freshly ground black pepper	

1. Cut beef into four thick slices. Set aside.
2. In a heavy nonstick skillet, heat oil on medium-high heat. Cook garlic for 30 seconds. Add beef and sauté on each side until brown and beef is still pink inside.
3. Add vinegar and salt and pepper to taste.

MENU SUGGESTION
- Crème Fraîche Mashed Potatoes (page 147) and Broiled Plum Tomatoes (page 155).

THAI BURGERS

Inspired by Asian flavors, these burgers are a hit whenever I serve them. You can choose between ground pork or beef — they both work. Fresh cilantro and chopped peanuts are great additions.

Makes 6		

TIP
Instead of lettuce on the buns, I use fresh cilantro leaves when I have them available.

1 lb	ground meat	500 g
3 tbsp	Asian Peanut Sauce (see recipe, page 122) or store-bought	45 mL
2	green onions, chopped	2
1 to 2 tsp	grated fresh gingerroot	5 to 10 mL
	Salt and freshly ground black pepper	

TIP
Instead of a hamburger bun, grill flat bread, toast country-style bread or slip the burger into a pita pocket.

1. In a bowl, combine meat, peanut sauce, onions, gingerroot, salt and pepper. Gently mix ingredients with a fork or your hands.

2. Divide into six equal amounts. Shape into thin patties. Cover and refrigerate or freeze for longer storage.

3. Cook patties for 5 to 7 minutes per side being careful that meat is no longer pink inside.

THAI BEEF SATAY

This is a very traditional recipe for a very traditional Thai dish. It can be served on small skewers for appetizers or on larger skewers for the main course. The Canadian Beef Information Center is the source of this recipe with only a modest change.

Serves 4

TIP
For a spicier version, add hot red pepper flakes and minced garlic to the peanut mixture.

• *PREHEAT BROILER OR BARBECUE*
• *WOODEN SKEWERS*

1 lb	fast fry or sirloin steak	500 g
¼ cup	peanut butter	50 mL
2 tbsp	soy sauce	25 mL
2 tbsp	freshly squeezed lime or lemon juice	25 mL
	Salt and freshly ground black pepper	

1. Cut beef into long strips about ½ inch (1 cm) wide. Set aside.

2. In a medium bowl, whisk together peanut butter, soy sauce, juice, 2 tbsp (25 mL) water, salt and pepper until smooth. Add beef strips and stir to coat. Let stand at room temperature for 15 minutes or refrigerate for several hours.

3. If using wooden skewers, soak them in cold water for at least 10 minutes to prevent charring during cooking.

4. Remove beef from peanut butter mixture. Thread strips loosely on skewers. Broil or grill for 4 minutes per side or until desired doneness and slightly pink inside. Serve at once.

BEEF AND VEGETABLE PACKAGES

Anyone who enjoys camping will find this recipe helpful.
It produces individual servings of meat and vegetables that
can be cooked in foil on a barbecue grill.

Serves 4

TIPS

You may want to add a few spoonfuls of red wine, tomato juice or water before closing the foil packages.

To check if cooked, unfold foil carefully on top. Pierce meat with a fork being careful the juices do not escape.

• *PREHEAT OVEN TO 350°F (180°C) OR GRILL TO MEDIUM-HIGH*

1 lb	blade or cross-rib steak, about 1 inch (2.5 cm) thick	500 g
1	large onion, cut into 8 wedges	1
2	potatoes, quartered	2
2	carrots, quartered	2
	Salt and freshly ground black pepper	

1. Sear meat on both sides on either a barbecue grill or in a skillet on the stove.

2. Place steak in center of a long length of heavy-duty foil. Arrange onion, potato and carrot on top of steak. Sprinkle lightly with salt and pepper (see Tip, left). You could also wrap in individual packets, which would be great for camping trips.

3. Wrap securely with double folds on top to prevent leakage. Bake seam-side up in preheated oven or grill for 30 minutes or until meat and vegetables are tender (see Tips, left). Turn package periodically during cooking especially if cooking on grill.

4. Remove meat and vegetables from foil, cut meat into four pieces and serve.

ONE-HOUR ONION BEEF ROAST

What a boon to the busy person — a roast that can be done in one hour!
This recipe gives you a tender, succulent roast. Part of the onion soup mix is
used with the meat — add the balance when making the gravy (see Tips, left).

Serves 6

TIPS

For gravy, add remaining soup mix to pan liquid, then thicken with a flour-water mix, approximately 2 tbsp (25 mL) flour and ¼ cup (50 mL) water.

If roast is larger than 3 lbs (1.5 kg), allow additional 10 minutes per 8 oz (250 g) at 325°F (160°C).

Variation

Other liquids, such as red wine, apple or tomato juice, can be heated and substituted for hot water.

- *PREHEAT OVEN TO 500°F (260°C)*
- *ROASTING PAN*

3 lbs	sirloin tip, rump or round roast (see Tips, left)	1.5 kg
1	pouch (1.5 oz/45 g) dried onion soup mix, divided	1
1	clove garlic, minced	1
½ tsp	dried thyme leaves	2 mL

1. Place roast in pan. Combine ¼ cup (50 mL) soup mix, garlic and thyme. Rub into roast.

2. Pour 2 cups (500 mL) hot water around meat. Bake in preheated oven, covered, for 20 minutes. Reduce heat to 325°F (160°C). Cook for 40 minutes more.

MENU SUGGESTION

- Caramelized Vidalia Onions (see recipe, page 161) and a tossed salad plus crusty whole wheat rolls complete the main course.

PORK CHOPS WITH CRANBERRIES

Cozy up the pork chops and cranberries in the oven with potatoes and squash for baking at the same time. Results — a warm and satisfying oven meal.

Serves 4	• PREHEAT OVEN TO 350°F (180°C) • 8-INCH (2 L) SQUARE OR ROUND BAKING DISH, GREASED		

4	pork chops, about 1 inch (2.5 cm) thick	4
	Salt and freshly ground black pepper	
1 cup	whole cranberries, fresh or frozen	250 mL
¼ cup	liquid honey	50 mL
¼ cup	red wine or stock	50 mL

1. Season chops lightly with salt and pepper. Arrange in prepared baking dish.

2. In a small bowl, combine cranberries, honey and wine. Stir well. Pour over chops.

3. Cover with foil and bake in preheated oven for 45 minutes. Remove foil. Continue baking for 10 minutes or until meat is tender.

POLYNESIAN PORK CHOPS

Sweet-and-sour sauce makes all the difference in speedy preparation of this dish. No need to make one from "scratch" because the sauce is readily available at the supermarket.

Serves 4	• PREHEAT OVEN TO 350°F (180°C) • 8-INCH (2 L) SQUARE OR ROUND BAKING DISH, GREASED		

Variation
Chicken pieces
work equally well.

4	pork chops, ¾ inch (2 cm) thick	4
	Salt and freshly ground black pepper	
1	green bell pepper, seeded and cut into cubes	1
1	medium onion, thinly sliced	1
1½ cups	sweet-and-sour sauce	375 mL

1. Season chops lightly with salt and pepper. Arrange in prepared baking dish. Top with green pepper and onion.

2. Pour sauce over top. Cover with foil and bake in preheated oven for 45 minutes. Remove foil. Continue baking for 10 minutes or until meat is tender.

MENU SUGGESTION

- Fluffy cooked brown or white rice and a green salad complete this quickly prepared dinner.

MARINATED PORK KEBABS

Beer makes a wonderful marinade for meats, especially pork kebabs. Add an assortment of vegetables to the skewers when you are grilling the meat, if desired.

Serves 4		

TIPS

Flat beer is preferable because it is less foamy.

Thread meat and vegetables on skewers with sufficient separation to allow even cooking.

The remaining one-quarter of marinade may be used to marinade any vegetables you are using. Any marinade in which raw meats have marinated should either be discarded or boiled for 5 minutes before further use to kill harmful bacteria.

• WOODEN SKEWERS

1	pork tenderloin (about 1 lb/500 g), cut into large cubes	1
1	bottle (12 oz/341 mL) beer (see Tips, left)	1
2	cloves garlic, minced	2
1 tbsp	dry mustard	15 mL
	Salt and freshly ground black pepper	

1. In a non-metallic dish, arrange pork cubes in a single layer. Whisk together beer, garlic and mustard. Pour three-quarters of mixture over the pork. Cover and let stand for 30 minutes at room temperature or overnight in the refrigerator.

2. If using wooden skewers, soak them in cold water for at least 10 minutes to prevent charring during cooking.

3. Remove pork and discard marinade. Thread meat (and vegetables, if using) onto skewers. Grill on preheated barbecue, turning occasionally, for 12 minutes or until a hint of pink remains inside. Brush meat and any vegetables with remaining marinade during grilling (see Tips, left).

RED-SAUCED PORK CHOPS

The Basic Red Tomato Sauce is especially wonderful for pork chops.
It adds so much flavor, while keeping the chops moist.
Complete the dinner with crusty rolls and a green vegetable.

<table>
<tr><td>Serves 4</td><td colspan="3"></td></tr>
</table>

TIP

Any of the sauce variations on page 120 may be used but it is especially nice to use the one with vegetables. It produces a more complete entrée.

4	pork chops, about 1 inch (2.5 cm) thick	4
1 cup	Basic Red Tomato Sauce (see recipe, page 120) or store-bought	250 mL
1 cup	long-grain white rice	250 mL
	Freshly grated Parmesan cheese or chopped parsley, optional	

1. Trim chops and discard fat. In a large Dutch oven or nonstick pan over medium heat, brown chops on each side, in batches as necessary. Return chops to pan.

2. Add sauce, 1 cup (250 mL) water and rice. Bring to a boil. Reduce heat to medium-low. Cover and cook for 25 minutes or until rice is tender and pork has just a hint of pink remaining.

3. Remove from heat. Cover and let stand for 5 minutes. Sprinkle with cheese or parsley, if using.

DIJON HAM STEAKS

Simple ham steak can be served at a dinner party dressed up
in a fresh fruity salsa such as Fresh Mango Salsa.

Serves 4

- *PREHEAT BROILER*
- *BAKING PAN, FOIL-LINED*

4	ham steaks (each 6 oz/180 g) or thick slices of ham	4
2 tbsp	Dijon mustard	25 mL
2 tbsp	packed brown sugar	25 mL
2 tbsp	pineapple or orange juice	25 mL
	Fresh Mango Salsa, optional (see recipe, page 75)	

1. Place ham on prepared pan. Score edges to prevent curling during broiling.

2. In a small bowl, stir together mustard, sugar and juice. Spread over meat.

3. Broil in preheated broiler for 5 minutes or until golden brown and glazed. Serve immediately with salsa, if using.

DIJON MUSTARD PORK MEDALLIONS

Sublime is the only way to describe pork served with this wonderfully creamy mustard sauce.

Serves 4

TIP

To serve sauce warm, place mixture in a heatproof measuring cup and warm in hot, not boiling, water for 3 minutes or until mixture is warm. Do not cook or it will curdle. Stir occasionally.

• NONSTICK COOKING SPRAY

1	pork tenderloin (about 1 lb/500 g), cut crosswise into 8 pieces	1
	Salt and freshly ground black pepper	
½ cup	plain yogurt or sour cream	125 mL
1 tbsp	Dijon mustard	15 mL
1	clove garlic, minced	1

1. Trim pork and discard fat. To make medallions, place pork, cut-side down, on a flat surface. Cover with waxed paper. Flatten gently with heel of hand, meat mallet or rolling pin to ¼ inch (1 cm) thick.

2. Heat nonstick skillet over medium-high heat. Lightly spray with cooking spray. Sauté medallions, in batches, for 3 minutes per side or until a hint of pink remains inside. Remove from skillet to a warm plate. Sprinkle lightly with salt and pepper.

3. In a small bowl, combine yogurt, mustard and garlic (see Tip, left). Serve a spoonful with each medallion.

MENU SUGGESTION

• Sauté of Spring Vegetables (see recipe, page 160) and basmati rice completes the menu.

TANGY ROASTED PORK TENDERLOIN

Cumin in combination with vinegar and brown sugar brings a zesty flavor to pork.

Serves 4		

• BAKING PAN, GREASED

1	pork tenderloin (about 1 lb/500 g)	1
¼ cup	packed brown sugar	50 mL
2 tbsp	cider vinegar	25 mL
1 tsp	ground cumin	5 mL
	Freshly ground black pepper	

1. Trim pork and discard fat. Set aside.

2. In a small bowl, combine sugar, vinegar, cumin and pepper. Add pork, turning to coat. Cover and refrigerate for 1 hour.

3. Remove pork from marinade. If reserving marinade to use as a glaze for the meat during cooking, place marinade in a small saucepan and boil for 5 minutes. You may need to add a small amount of water.

4. Place pork in prepared pan. Roast in 375°F (190°C) oven for 30 minutes or until meat thermometer registers 160°F (70°C). Remove from oven. Tent with foil and let stand 5 minutes. Cut into slices. Drizzle with juices from pan.

MENU SUGGESTION

• Add Scalloped Vegetable Casserole (see recipe, page 154) and whole wheat rolls for an easy weeknight dinner.

MARMALADE-GLAZED PORK ROAST

Citrus-flavored marmalade is a fine accompaniment to pork. Use with either pork roast or tenderloin. With tenderloin, brush it on before roasting. With a longer-cooking, larger roast, brush on during the last half-hour.

Serves 6 **Makes about** **½ cup** **(125 mL) glaze**		

• PREHEAT OVEN TO 325°F (160°C)
• SHALLOW BAKING PAN, FOIL-LINED

1	pork roast (about 3 lbs/1.5 kg)	1
½ cup	melted orange marmalade	125 mL
1 tbsp	mustard	15 mL
1 tbsp	chopped fresh rosemary	15 mL
	Salt and freshly ground black pepper	

1. Trim pork and discard fat. Set aside.

2. In a small bowl, stir together marmalade, mustard, rosemary, salt and pepper. Brush half on meat. Set remaining glaze aside.

3. Arrange meat in prepared pan. Roast in preheated oven for 20 to 25 minutes per pound, basting twice with reserved glaze, or until a meat thermometer registers 160°F (70°C). Remove from oven. Tent with foil and let stand for 5 minutes. Cut into slices. Drizzle with juices from pan.

MENU SUGGESTION

• Skillet-Style Onion and Sweet Potatoes (see recipe, page 146) and a green salad complement each other and the pork.

SPECIAL LAMB MARINADES

Marinating and basting are two of the great techniques used in meat cookery. The following three marinades enhance the succulent lamb flavor. Most of the ingredients are probably already in your pantry. Each recipe is sufficient for an 8-rib rack of lamb or a 5 lb (2.5 kg) leg. The result is succulent meat with a great flavor.

Makes ⅔ cup (150 mL)

SOY HONEY LEMON

¼ cup	liquid honey	50 mL
¼ cup	freshly squeezed lemon juice	50 mL
¼ cup	soy sauce	50 mL
I	large clove garlic, crushed	I
	Freshly ground black pepper	

1. In a small bowl, combine honey, lemon juice, soy sauce, garlic and pepper.

2. Place meat in a large plastic bag. Pour marinade over meat, seal bag securely and refrigerate overnight for a marvelous flavor when meat is cooked.

Makes about ⅓ cup (75 mL)

MUSTARD AND HERB

3 tbsp	coarse mustard	45 mL
2 tbsp	chopped fresh tarragon or I tbsp (15 mL) dried	25 mL
2 tbsp	chopped fresh chives	25 mL
2 tbsp	olive oil	25 mL

1. In a small bowl, stir together mustard, tarragon, chives and oil.

2. Brush surface of meat with mixture. Cover meat and refrigerate for several hours before cooking.

Makes about ⅓ cup (75 mL)

CLASSIC ROSEMARY AND GARLIC

3 tbsp	Worcestershire sauce	45 mL
2 tbsp	coarsely chopped fresh rosemary or I tbsp (15 mL) dried	25 mL
2 tbsp	olive oil	25 mL
4	cloves garlic, sliced	4

1. In a small bowl, combine Worcestershire sauce, rosemary and oil.

2. Insert slivers of garlic into cuts in lamb. Brush surface with rosemary mixture. Cover meat and refrigerate for several hours before cooking.

TO COOK BONE-IN LEG OF LAMB

- Place lamb on rack in a roasting pan or on barbecue grill. Roast at 350°F (180°C) for 18 minutes per pound (500 g) or until meat thermometer registers 150°F (65°C) at thickest part of meat. Transfer to a warm plate and let rest for 10 minutes before carving.

TO GRILL BUTTERFLIED BONELESS LEG OF LAMB

- Grill on medium heat, about 4 to 6 inches (10 to 15 cm) from heat. Turn lamb occasionally, basting with any reserved marinade. Cook, covered, for 12 minutes per pound (500 g) for medium or until browned but still pink in the center or until meat thermometer registers 150°F (65°C) at thickest part of meat.

- Transfer to a warm plate and let rest for 10 minutes before carving.

TO COOK RACK OF LAMB

- Sear both sides of rack in a skillet over high heat until brown. Place in roasting pan and let cool. (Lamb can be prepared to this point and refrigerated for up to one day.) Season lightly with salt and pepper. Roast meat in 400°F (200°C) oven, fat-side up, for 10 to 15 minutes per pound (500 g) for rare and 15 to 18 minutes for medium. Transfer to a warm plate and let rest for 10 minutes before carving.

LAMB SOUVLAKI

The usual meat for this Greek favorite is lamb, although I also like it with pork. Either way, chunks of meat are marinated in a lemon juice, oil and herb mixture before being skewered and grilled. Vegetable chunks, such as green pepper or onion, can be added.

Serves 4

SAFETY TIP
If you are basting with the lemon marinade in which the raw meat has been marinating, bring it to a boil for 5 minutes to kill any harmful bacteria left from marinating raw meat.

Pork Variation
Boneless pork loin or tenderloin may replace the lamb.

• *WOODEN SKEWERS*

1 lb	lean boneless lamb	500 g
¼ cup	freshly squeezed lemon juice	50 mL
¼ cup	olive oil	50 mL
2 to 4	cloves garlic, minced	2 to 4
	Salt and freshly ground black pepper	

1. Trim lamb and discard fat. Cut into 1-inch (2.5 cm) chunks. Set aside.

2. In a bowl, whisk together lemon juice, oil, garlic, salt and pepper. Add meat and stir to coat. Marinate for up to 24 hours in the refrigerator or at room temperature for 30 minutes.

3. If using wooden skewers, soak them in cold water for at least 10 minutes to prevent charring during cooking.

4. Remove meat from marinade. Reserve marinade for basting (see Safety Tip, left).

5. Thread meat on four skewers. Broil under preheated broiler 6 inches (15 cm) from heat. Turn and baste halfway through with cooked marinade. Or grill on preheated broiler over medium-high heat for 5 minutes per side for rare and 7 minutes per side for medium.

SERVING SUGGESTION

• Tzatziki (see recipe, page 23) is well worth making as it complements lamb so well. Stuff cooked meat and Tzatziki into an open pita pocket for a memorable meal.

CLASSIC MARINADES

Having a supply of any of these marinades in the refrigerator makes fast work of marinating meats and vegetables. As well, I find them very useful as salad dressing vinaigrettes. Inspiration for the recipes comes from the Canola Information Service, Saskatchewan, Canada.

Makes about 1/3 cup (75 mL)

TIP
Use with pork chops or chicken breasts.

HONEY GARLIC MARINADE

1/4 cup	liquid honey	50 mL
2 tbsp	light soy sauce	25 mL
2 tsp	canola oil	10 mL
2	cloves garlic, minced	2

1. In a tightly covered container, combine all ingredients. Shake until well blended. Use immediately or store in the refrigerator until needed. It will keep for several weeks.

Makes about 2/3 cup (150 mL)

TIP
Use with pork chops, chicken breasts or beef.

PRAIRIE BARBECUE MARINADE

1/4 cup	beer	50 mL
1/4 cup	Dijon mustard	50 mL
2 tbsp	canola oil	25 mL
2 tbsp	liquid honey	25 mL
	Freshly ground black pepper, to taste	

1. In a tightly covered container, combine all ingredients. Shake until well blended. Use immediately or store in the refrigerator until needed. It will keep for several weeks.

Makes about 1/2 cup (125 mL)

TIP
Use with fish, pork tenderloin, chicken or lamb.

THAI MARINADE

1/4 cup	light soy sauce	50 mL
2 tbsp	canola oil	25 mL
2 tbsp	rice vinegar	25 mL
1 tbsp	minced fresh gingerroot	15 mL
	Freshly ground black pepper, to taste	

1. In a tightly covered container, combine all ingredients. Shake until well blended. Use immediately or store in the refrigerator until needed. It will keep for several weeks.

HERBAL MARINADE

Marinades are an indispensable part of cooking, especially on a grill. The addition of a few tasty herbs adds to their appeal. While marinades can be used to tenderize meats, it's their ability to impart subtle flavors to everything from fish to vegetables that makes them such a favorite with cooks.

Makes ⅓ cup (75 mL)

TIP
Use with beef or pork.

Variations
Oregano substituted for basil is excellent with beef or as a drizzle over sliced tomatoes.

Dill substituted for basil is perfect for fish or chicken.

¼ cup	finely chopped fresh basil leaves (see Variations, left)	50 mL
2	cloves garlic, minced	2
	Zest and juice of 1 lime	
2 tbsp	vegetable oil	25 mL
	Salt and freshly ground black pepper	

1. In a small bowl, combine basil, garlic, lime juice and zest, oil, salt and pepper.

2. Use immediately or store for up to 3 days in a tightly sealed container in the refrigerator until ready to use as a marinade.

PASTA, RICE & GRAINS

MOST OF US LEAD PRETTY HECTIC LIVES AND SOMETIMES THE LAST THING we feel like doing at the end of the day is making dinner. Instead, stop at your local deli counter, pick up whatever you fancy, maybe a roasted chicken, and serve it with one of the fast side dishes in this chapter.

Pasta is budget-friendly and extends more expensive foods. It is the ideal basic food — rich in complex carbohydrates, high in protein and low in fat. It only becomes fattening from what you put on it. A 2-cup (500 mL) serving of pasta provides up to 14 grams of incomplete protein, about one-third of the daily requirement.

While rice is common in North America, half the world eats rice as its staple food. Although there are more than 7,000 varieties of rice grown, they all fall into three general categories, short, medium and long-grain.

Grains and grain products — flour, bread, cereal and pasta — are the chief forms of sustenance in most countries of the world. Whole grains are rich in fiber and an inexpensive and a readily available source of low-fat protein. Grains also contain more carbohydrates than any other food.

BASIC RED TOMATO SAUCE

Dinner preparation is a cinch with a supply of this sauce in the refrigerator or freezer. See Index (page 187) for more uses for this great sauce.

Makes 5 cups (1.25 L)		
1	can (28 oz/796 mL) diced tomatoes	1
1	can (5½ oz/156 mL) tomato paste	1
2	large onions, chopped	2
2	cloves garlic, minced	2
	Salt and freshly ground black pepper	

Variations
Add any of these additions to 1 cup (250 mL) sauce.

Mushroom Sauce
1 can (10 oz/284 mL) drained mushrooms.

Vegetable Sauce
½ diced green or red bell pepper, ½ diced zucchini or 1 cup (250 mL) chopped broccoli and 1 stalk celery chopped.

1. In a large saucepan, combine tomatoes, tomato paste, onions, garlic and ¾ cup (175 mL) water. Bring to a boil on medium-high heat. Reduce heat to medium-low and cook, uncovered, stirring frequently, for 1 hour or until mixture is cooked and thickened. Add additional water if sauce becomes too thick. Season with salt and pepper to taste.

2. Remove from heat. Let cool before storing in smaller containers. Freeze for longer storage or refrigerate for about 2 days.

ROASTED RED PEPPER PASTA SAUCE

Keep a jar of roasted red peppers on hand to make this gorgeous sauce. Better yet, roast your own when they are in season and freeze them.

Makes 1 cup (250 mL)		
1	jar (10½ oz/313 mL) roasted red peppers, drained (see Tip, above right)	1
1 tbsp	olive oil	15 mL
2	cloves garlic, minced	2
1 tsp	dried oregano leaves or 1 tbsp (15 mL) chopped fresh oregano	5 mL
	Salt and freshly ground black pepper	

1. In a food processor, purée red peppers. Set aside.

2. Heat oil in a nonstick skillet over medium heat. Add garlic and oregano. Cook, stirring, for 30 seconds.

3. Add pepper purée. Reduce heat and cook slowly for 2 minutes. Season with salt and pepper to taste. Store in refrigerator for one week or freeze for longer storage.

4. Serve the sauce over cooked pasta. As a final touch, you can sprinkle the cooked sauce and pasta with some grated Parmigiano-Reggiano cheese at serving time.

TUNA TOMATO PASTA TOSS

Our Basic Red Tomato Sauce, a can of tuna, some pasta and a frozen vegetable make a quick dinner. Put a salad together while the pasta is cooking.

Serves 4

Variation
Any frozen vegetable, such as corn, mixed vegetables, carrots or green beans, work well here.

8 oz	penne, fusilli or spaghetti	250 g
2 cups	Basic Red Tomato Sauce (see recipe, page 120) or store-bought	500 mL
1	can (6½ oz/170 g) tuna, water packed, drained	1
1 cup	frozen peas (see Variation, left)	250 mL
	Freshly ground black pepper	

1. In a large saucepan of boiling water, cook pasta according to package directions until al dente (tender but firm). Drain well. Return to saucepan.

2. Add sauce, tuna and peas. Cook on low for 5 minutes or until sauce is hot and peas are heated. Season with pepper to taste.

ASIAN PEANUT SAUCE

Peanut butter is a guaranteed pantry staple in my house. This sauce will also become another pantry staple to enjoy in other recipes.

Makes 2½ cups (675 mL)			
1	jar (16 oz/500 g) creamy peanut butter	1
1 to 2	cloves garlic, minced	1 to 2
¼ cup	soy sauce	50 mL
2 tsp	sesame oil	10 mL
	Salt and freshly ground black pepper	

1. In a medium saucepan, over medium-low heat, heat peanut butter, garlic, soy sauce and sesame oil, stirring frequently, for 10 minutes or until smooth and melted.

2. Season with salt and pepper to taste. Spoon into tightly covered container and refrigerate for several days until ready to use.

EGG NOODLES WITH PEANUT SAUCE

The versatile Asian Peanut Sauce comes in handy here. This is a fast and delicious vegetarian recipe.

Serves 4		
2 cups	egg noodles	500 mL
1 cup	snow peas, trimmed	250 mL
2	green onions, sliced on the diagonal	2
½ cup	Asian Peanut Sauce (see recipe, above) or store-bought	125 mL
	Salt and freshly ground black pepper	

1. In a large saucepan, cook egg noodles in boiling water according to package directions.

2. Add snow peas during last few minutes of cooking. Drain well and return to saucepan.

3. Stir green onions and Asian Peanut Sauce into pasta. Season with salt and pepper to taste.

PASTA WITH VEGETABLES AND PEANUT SAUCE

With the Asian Peanut Sauce, a few vegetables and a salad, you have an ideal vegetarian meal.

Serves 4

TIPS
Different vegetables may be used here. I especially like short pieces of asparagus or small broccoli florets.

During the tossing of cooked pasta and peanut sauce, you may wish to add a small amount of sesame oil to keep the pasta from becoming too sticky.

12 oz	fresh linguine pasta	375 g
½	red bell pepper, cut into thin strips	½
1	medium carrot, peeled and cut into thin strips (see Tips, left)	1
½ cup	Asian Peanut Sauce (see recipe, left) or store-bought	125 mL
	Salt and freshly ground black pepper	

1. In a large saucepan, cook pasta in boiling water according to package directions.

2. Add red pepper and carrots during last few minutes of cooking. Drain well and return to saucepan.

3. Stir Asian Peanut Sauce into pasta. Season with salt and pepper to taste.

COUSCOUS WITH VEGETABLES

Couscous, a staple of North African cuisine, is my all-time favorite to serve with a spicy meal. It is also a great alternative to rice.

Serves 6		

2 cups	chicken stock	500 mL
¾ cup	frozen mixed vegetables	175 mL
1¼ cups	couscous	300 mL
¼ cup	slivered almonds, toasted	50 mL

1. In a medium saucepan over high heat, bring stock to a boil. Add vegetables. Cook for 3 minutes. Add couscous and stir.

2. Remove from heat. Cover and let stand for 5 minutes or until liquid is absorbed. Fluff with a fork and stir in almonds.

SERVING SUGGESTIONS

- This makes a great filling for green or red bell peppers which can then be baked.
- Serve with Indian Chicken Kebabs (see recipe, page 83) to complete the meal.

MAC 'N' CHEESE NIGHT

Wonder what to have for dinner tonight? This classic favorite from all of our childhood food memories may just be the answer.

Serves 4		

2 cups	macaroni or fusilli	500 mL
3 tbsp	butter or margarine	45 mL
1½ cups	shredded Cheddar cheese	375 mL
¾ cup	sour cream	175 mL
	Salt and freshly ground black pepper	

Tomato Cheese Variation
Replace sour cream with ¾ cup (175 mL) diced tomatoes, either fresh or canned.

1. In a medium saucepan of boiling water, cook macaroni according to package directions until al dente (tender but firm). Drain well. Return to saucepan.

2. Remove from heat and stir in butter until melted. Stir in cheese, adding a small amount at a time. Add sour cream and salt and pepper to taste. Stir until pasta is well coated with sauce and cheese is melted.

BROCCOLI AND RED ONION PASTA

Cook small florets of broccoli along with the pasta during the last few minutes of cooking.

Serves 4		
2 tbsp	olive oil	25 mL
1	medium red onion, thinly sliced	1
1	package (12 oz/375 g) pasta, such as rotini or fusilli	1
2 cups	broccoli florets	500 mL
	Freshly grated Parmesan cheese, for garnish, optional	

1. Heat oil in a small skillet over medium heat. Cook onion, stirring frequently, for 3 minutes or until softened. Set aside.

2. In a large saucepan of boiling water, cook pasta according to package directions or until al dente (tender but firm). Add broccoli and cook until just tender.

3. Ladle ¼ cup (50 mL) pasta water into a large serving bowl. Drain pasta and broccoli and add to serving bowl. Add onion and toss with Parmesan cheese, if using. Serve immediately.

PEROGY CASSEROLE

*I remember this casserole becoming a real favorite with my young
children — and with me, as well. It was so easy to make and so tasty to eat.*

Serves 4 to 6		

TIP
You may need extra
liquid if contents
of casserole are too
thick. Either use
water or milk; about
¼ cup (50 mL)
should be enough.

- PREHEAT OVEN TO 350°F (180°C)
- 8-CUP (2 L) DEEP CASSEROLE, GREASED

I lb	fresh or frozen perogies	500 g
I	can (10 oz/284 mL) condensed mushroom soup, undiluted	I
I cup	shredded Cheddar cheese	250 mL
I	large onion, chopped	I
	Freshly ground black pepper	

1. In a large bowl, combine perogies, mushroom soup, cheese, onion and pepper. Stir to combine. Transfer to prepared casserole dish.

2. Bake in preheated oven, covered, for 35 minutes for fresh perogies or 50 minutes, if using frozen, or until hot, bubbling and cheese has melted.

MUSHROOM BAKED RICE

*Rice is absolutely foolproof when cooked in the oven — and
the temptation to peek by lifting the lid is more difficult.*

Serves 4		

- PREHEAT OVEN TO 400°F (200°C)
- 6-CUP (1.5 L) CASSEROLE, GREASED

I tbsp	olive oil	15 mL
I cup	sliced mushrooms (any variety)	250 mL
I cup	long-grain rice	250 mL
I½ cups	hot chicken or beef stock	375 mL
	Freshly ground black pepper	

1. In a nonstick skillet, heat oil over medium-high heat. Add mushrooms. Sauté for 5 minutes. Stir in rice and stock.

2. Transfer to prepared casserole. Cover and bake in preheated oven for 20 minutes or until liquid is absorbed and rice is tender. Let stand for 5 minutes before serving. Season with pepper to taste.

RICE PILAF WITH TOASTED ALMONDS

Pilaf originated in the Near East. It can be served as a main or side dish. I prefer this dish with nutty-tasting brown rice but you can use white rice, if your family prefers it. Remember, white rice cooks in less time than brown, which takes about 40 minutes.

Serves 8		
2 tbsp	olive oil	25 mL
1	medium onion, finely chopped	1
1 ½ cups	brown rice	375 mL
	Freshly ground black pepper	
½ cup	sliced almonds, toasted (see Tip, left)	125 mL

TIP
To toast almonds, place in a small microwave-safe dish, cook on High for 1 minute or until nuts are golden brown.

Variations

Saffron Rice
Add a pinch of saffron threads to the rice and water during cooking. It provides a wonderfully pungent flavor.

Dried Fruit
Add ⅓ to ½ cup (75 to 125 mL) currants or diced dried apricots or prunes.

Chicken or beef stock can replace water.

1. In a large saucepan, heat oil over medium heat. Cook onion, stirring, until light brown. Add rice and stir for 2 minutes. Add 3 cups (750 mL) water (see Variations, left). Bring to a boil. Reduce heat to low. Cover and cook for 40 minutes or until all liquid is absorbed and rice is tender.

2. Fluff rice with a fork. Add pepper to taste and almonds before serving.

SAFFRON NOTE

- It's no wonder that saffron is the world's most expensive spice. It comes from the stigma of a small purple crocus. Each flower provides only three stigmas, which are carefully handpicked and dried. It takes more than 14,000 of these tiny stigmas to make an ounce of saffron. It is a good thing a little goes a long way!

CHEESY RICE CASSEROLE

This dairy-rich casserole, along with a salad and fruit for dessert,
provides a light, nutritious but no less satisfying meal.

Serves 6		

- PREHEAT OVEN TO 400°F (200°C)
- 6-CUP (1.5 L) CASSEROLE, GREASED

2 cups	vegetable or chicken stock	500 mL
¾ cup	long-grain brown rice	175 mL
I cup	light sour cream	250 mL
I cup	cottage cheese	250 mL
	Salt and freshly ground black pepper	

1. In a large saucepan, bring stock to a boil. Add rice. Cover and cook on low heat for 20 minutes or until rice is tender and liquid is absorbed. Let stand for 5 minutes.

2. Combine rice, sour cream, cottage cheese, salt and pepper. Spoon into prepared casserole. Bake in preheated oven, uncovered, for 20 minutes or until heated.

SPICED MICROWAVE BASMATI RICE

Much valued in India and Middle Eastern kitchens,
basmati rice offers exciting opportunities for cooks. Prepare it
in the microwave oven for true "no-stick, no-peek" cooking.

Serves 6		

Variation
You can substitute the water with such liquids as beef, chicken or vegetable stock for additional and different flavors.

- 8-CUP (2 L) MICROWAVE-SAFE CONTAINER

I cup	basmati rice	250 mL
I tbsp	vegetable oil	15 mL
I cup	chopped onion	250 mL
2 tbsp	finely chopped gingerroot	25 mL

recipe continues on page 129

Couscous with Vegetables *(page 124)* ▶
Overleaf: Vegetable Pizza *(page 136)*

Variation
For extra spicing,
add a couple of
cinnamon sticks and
a few whole cloves.
Remove them before
you serve the rice.

1. Rinse rice under cold running water until water is clear. Set aside.

2. In microwave-safe container, microwave oil and onions on High for 3 minutes. Add rice, 3 cups (750 mL) water (see Variation, page 128) and gingerroot. Cover and microwave on High for 8 minutes or until boiling. Stir.

3. Reduce to Medium-High. Cover and cook for 20 minutes or until all liquid is absorbed and rice is tender. Stir twice. Allow rice to stand for 10 minutes before serving.

SUN-DRIED TOMATO QUINOA

Quinoa is a grain from Peru that contains more protein than any other grain. In fact, it is considered to be the "supergrain of the future."

Serves 4			
I cup	quinoa (see Tip, left)		250 mL
2 tbsp	chopped dry-packed sun-dried tomatoes		25 mL
2	cloves garlic, minced		2
2 cups	chicken stock		500 mL
	Salt and freshly ground black pepper		

TIP
Quinoa may be fairly new to our markets, but it is actually a staple of the ancient Incas, who called it "the mother grain." It remains to this day an important food in South American cuisine. It can be found in most health food stores and in some supermarkets.

1. Rinse quinoa under cold running water until water is clear. Set aside.

2. Soak tomatoes for 10 minutes in boiling water. Drain and chop. Set aside.

3. In a medium saucepan, combine quinoa, tomatoes, garlic and stock. Bring to a boil. Cover, reduce heat and cook for 25 minutes or until all liquid is absorbed and quinoa is tender. Season with salt and pepper to taste.

CREAMY POLENTA

Polenta is a staple of northern Italian cuisine. The Food Lover's Companion describes it as *"mush made from cornmeal,"* an apt description except that it tastes better than you could ever imagine mush tasting. This version adds cream cheese to provide extra creaminess. It can be served as a main course or side dish and makes hearty breakfast fare.

	Serves 6	

TIP
You can replace the cream cheese with either Gorgonzola or the authentic Parmigiano-Reggiano.

2 tbsp	olive oil	25 mL
2	cloves garlic, minced	2
¼ cup	cream cheese (see Tip, left)	50 mL
1 cup	cornmeal	250 mL
	Salt and freshly ground black pepper	

1. In a large saucepan, heat oil over medium heat. Cook garlic, stirring, for 1 minute until softened.

2. Add 5 cups (1.25 L) water. Bring to a boil. Whisk in cream cheese until melted.

3. Gradually whisk in cornmeal. Cook, stirring constantly, until beginning to thicken. Reduce heat to low. Cook cornmeal, stirring frequently, for 30 minutes or until cornmeal is thickened and no longer grainy. Season with salt and pepper to taste.

BASIC CREAMY RISOTTO

Risotto originates in the rice-growing area of northern Italy. It has to be made with a plump, short-grained rice such as Arborio. When cooked, it is delectably creamy with separate and firm grains. It must be served immediately after cooking to be at its best. Serve as an accompaniment to your main course or on its own as the Italians often do. See the several variations below.

Serves 4 to 6

1 tbsp	olive oil	15 mL
½ cup	chopped onion	125 mL
1 cup	Arborio rice	250 mL
3 cups	hot chicken stock	750 mL
	Salt and freshly ground black pepper	

Variations

Squash
Add 1 cup (250 mL) mashed squash when the rice is almost tender with a pinch of freshly ground nutmeg.

Cheese
Add ¼ cup (50 mL) freshly grated Parmesan cheese near the end of cooking.

Mushroom
Sauté 2 cups (500 mL) sliced mushrooms of any type in a small amount of olive oil until golden. Adding soaked, dried porcini mushrooms would be very Italian.

1. Heat oil in a large saucepan over medium heat. Add onion and cook, stirring, for 3 minutes until soft. Add rice and cook, stirring, for 2 minutes until rice is coated with oil.

2. Add stock, ½ cup (125 mL) at a time, stirring often. (A small amount of white wine may be substituted for some of the stock.) Wait until liquid is absorbed before adding more stock. (It is this process that produces the creaminess.)

3. When all stock is used and rice is nearly tender, season with salt and pepper to taste. Serve immediately. (It is at this time that extras such as squash or cheese are added; see Variations, left).

BASIL PESTO SAUCE

Be sure to make lots of pesto when the garden is full of fresh basil.
Freeze what you can't use. This classic sauce has many uses
beyond pastas, including Mediterranean Chicken (see recipe, page 89)
and Polenta Pie (see recipe, page 20) as well as a host of many variations
which appear below. You can also use store-bought pesto.

Makes 2 cups (500 mL)		
3 cups	packed fresh basil leaves	750 mL
2	cloves garlic	2
1/3 cup	extra virgin olive oil	75 mL
1/3 cup	slivered almonds or pine nuts	75 mL
1/3 cup	freshly grated Parmesan cheese, optional	75 mL

Variations

Bruschetta
Spread some sauce over thick slices of Italian bread. Broil for 2 to 3 minutes or until just bubbling and starting to brown. For extra color, add diced tomatoes.

Pesto Dip
Stir 1 to 2 tsp (5 to 10 mL) sauce into sour cream or plain yogurt. Serve with vegetable crudités.

Pesto Pasta
Toss some sauce with hot cooked pasta.

Pesto Vinaigrette Dressing
Combine 1/3 cup (75 mL) olive oil, 2 tbsp (25 mL) white wine vinegar and 1 tbsp (15 mL) sauce.

1. In a food processor or blender, process basil, garlic, oil and almonds until coarsely chopped.

2. Add cheese, if using, and process until well mixed.

3. *To freeze:* At the end of Step 1, freeze the mixture in small amounts. When you remove it from the freezer to thaw, add the cheese and then use the pesto in one of the recipes, left.

VEGETARIAN DISHES

VEGETARIAN DISHES ARE PROTEIN-RICH FOODS THAT GENERALLY HAVE less fat than is associated with the traditional proteins of meats, fish and poultry. They include dairy products, eggs, tofu and other soy products, legumes, such as beans and lentils, grains, nuts and seeds. These foods can provide variety in our diets, often at less cost. The lentils and grains are especially high in fiber.

Plant products, which include soy foods, are the hot topic today. There are some very exciting facts. Unlike other plant proteins, soy products are complete proteins. That means that, like meats, poultry and fish, they contain all nine essential amino acids, the building blocks needed for growth and repair of our bodies.

Soybeans and soy products are nutritionally superior to other legumes because they have significant amounts of phytochemicals such as isoflavones. Phytochemicals are naturally occurring substances found in plants and have been linked to good health. For example, soy's isoflavones appear to reduce cancer risk and heart disease by lowering blood cholesterol. Soy protein has been found to be effective in treating kidney disease and may cause calcium to be better utilized, helping to ward off osteoporosis. Soybeans and soy products, such as tofu, also provide significant dietary protein without the saturated fat of animal-based products.

BLACK BEAN CHILI

The ready availability of canned black beans makes for
a quick and easy preparation of this excellent chili.

Serves 4		
I	onion, chopped	I
2	tomatoes, chopped	2
I	can (19 oz/540 mL) black beans, drained and rinsed	I
I tbsp	chili powder	15 mL
	Salt and freshly ground black pepper	

1. In a medium saucepan, covered, combine onion, tomatoes, black beans and chili powder. Bring to a boil. Reduce heat and cook for 20 minutes or until vegetables are tender.

2. Season with salt and pepper to taste.

SERVING SUGGESTION

• We enjoy eating chili with whole wheat toast or crusty rolls. Add a salad for a simple, satisfying meal.

BLACK BEAN PASTA SAUCE

Serve this great vegetarian sauce with cooked pasta,
ravioli, perogies or alone with crusty rolls.

Serves 6		
I	can (28 oz/796 mL) diced tomatoes	I
I	can (19 oz/540 mL) black beans, drained and rinsed (see Tip, left)	I
½ cup	packed cilantro leaves	125 mL
2 tbsp	balsamic vinegar	25 mL
	Freshly ground black pepper	

TIP
Rinsing beans lowers the sodium and gives them a less cloudy appearance. And very few nutrients are lost.

1. In a medium saucepan, combine tomatoes, beans, cilantro, vinegar and pepper to taste. Bring to a boil. Reduce heat and cook slowly, uncovered, for 20 minutes or until mixture is thickened.

TOMATO-BAKED BEAN CASSEROLE

Using cooked beans, either canned or home cooked, is a fast and easy way to make this old-fashioned casserole.

Serves 4

TIP
The Quick Soak method (see below) is the most efficient way to prepare dried beans. Use it for any dried bean including soybeans, white navy, kidney or pinto beans. It only takes one hour and works just as well as soaking overnight — but remember, whichever method you choose, discard the water the beans are soaked in and start with fresh water when you are ready to cook them.

• PREHEAT OVEN TO 325°F (160°C)
• 6-CUP (1.5 L) CASSEROLE

½ cup	finely chopped onions	125 mL
1	can (19 oz/540 mL) white beans, drained (see Tip, left)	1
1	can (10 oz/284 mL) stewed tomatoes	1
¼ cup	firmly packed brown sugar	50 mL

1. In a casserole, combine onion, beans, tomatoes and sugar. Stir well.
2. Cover and bake in preheated oven for 45 minutes, checking occasionally to see if the mixture is too dry, and adding a little water, if needed.

COOKING WITH DRIED BEANS

- *Quick Soak:* In a large saucepan, cover dry beans with cold water. Cover and bring to a boil. Reduce heat and cook slowly for 5 minutes. Remove from heat. Let stand for 1 hour. Drain and discard liquid.
- *Final Cooking:* After quick soaking, again cover beans with cold water. Bring to a boil. Cover and reduce heat. Cook for 1½ hours or until beans are tender. Add more water as necessary.

MARGHERITA PIZZA

This pizza uses a packaged plain pizza shell, tomatoes, some cheese and rosemary. It's a very traditional simple pizza that appears on all menus in Italy.

Serves 4

TIP
To replace rosemary, add chopped fresh or dried basil leaves or oregano as a topping for the pizza.

• *PREHEAT OVEN TO 375°F (190°C)*
• *LARGE BAKING SHEET, LIGHTLY GREASED*

1	plain Italian flatbread crust or pizza shell (14 oz/400 g)	1
1 cup	shredded mozzarella cheese	250 mL
2	ripe tomatoes, thinly sliced	2
	Fresh rosemary, chopped (see Tip, left)	

1. Place crust on prepared baking sheet. Sprinkle cheese over crust.

2. Arrange tomatoes in overlapping slices over cheese. Sprinkle liberally with rosemary.

3. Bake in preheated oven for 12 minutes or until cheese has melted and tomatoes are partially cooked. Cut into 4 wedges and serve.

VEGETABLE PIZZA

One portion of the Basic Red Tomato Sauce is the magic ingredient when making this fast pizza. Top with assorted vegetables, add cheese and a sprinkling of an Italian herb and dinner is on the table faster than it would arrive by pizza delivery.

Serves 4

Pizza Variation
Greek Pizza
Sliced black olives, crumbled feta cheese, sprinkling of dried oregano and chopped artichokes.

• *PREHEAT OVEN TO 375°F (190°C)*
• *LARGE BAKING SHEET, LIGHTLY GREASED*

1	plain Italian flatbread crust or pizza shell (14 oz/400 g)	1
1 cup	Basic Red Tomato Sauce (see recipe, page 120) or store-bought	250 mL
1 cup	bell peppers in assorted colors, cut into bite-size pieces (see Vegetable Suggestions, top right)	250 mL
1 cup	shredded Cheddar or mozzarella cheese	250 mL

Pizza Variation

Asian Fusion
Sliced bamboo shoots, mushrooms, water chestnuts and green onions. Drizzle of soy or teriyaki sauce and skip the cheese.

1. Place crust on prepared baking sheet. Spread evenly with tomato sauce. Top with bell peppers or other assorted vegetables (see suggestions below). Sprinkle with cheese.

2. Bake in preheated oven for 12 minutes or until heated and cheese is melted. Cut into 4 wedges and serve.

VEGETABLE SUGGESTIONS

- Sliced mushrooms, cooked broccoli or cauliflower florets, sliced red onion, sliced green onions or zucchini.

CARAMELIZED ONION AND GOAT CHEESE PIZZA

Packaged plain pizza shells take most of the work out of home pizza preparation. Since this pizza has a gourmet touch, guests will enjoy it for a casual supper.

Serves 4

- PREHEAT OVEN TO 375°F (190°C)
- LARGE BAKING SHEET, LIGHTLY GREASED

1	plain Italian flatbread crust or pizza shell (14 oz/400 g)	1
1 tbsp	olive oil	15 mL
2 cups	thinly sliced onion, separated into rings	500 mL
⅔ cup	crumbled goat cheese	150 mL

1. Place crust on prepared baking sheet.

2. In a nonstick skillet, heat oil over medium-high heat. Cook onion, covered, for 3 minutes. Uncover and cook, stirring often, for 10 minutes or until golden brown.

3. Spread onions over crust. Top with cheese. Bake in preheated oven for 12 minutes or until heated and cheese is melted. Cut into 4 wedges and serve.

SPINACH CRUSTLESS QUICHE

*A wonderful lunch or vegetarian dinner, this crustless quiche is
an excellent source of calcium and a good source of iron. Add
a simple salad and some crusty rolls to complete the meal.*

| Serves 4 | • PREHEAT OVEN TO 325°F (160°C)
• 10-INCH (25 CM) PIE PLATE, GREASED | |
|---|---|---|

1	package (10 oz/300 g) frozen chopped spinach, thawed	1
1	red bell pepper, finely chopped	1
4	eggs	4
1 cup	cottage cheese	250 mL
	Salt and freshly ground black pepper	

1. Drain spinach by pressing out moisture with a slotted spoon. Spread half in prepared pie plate. Sprinkle with red pepper.

2. In a large bowl, beat eggs and cottage cheese. Add salt and pepper to taste. Stir in remaining spinach. Pour into pie plate.

3. Bake in preheated oven for 40 minutes or until knife inserted in center comes out clean. Remove from oven. Let stand for 5 minutes before cutting into 4 wedges.

QUINOA VEGETABLE STIR-FRY

*Quinoa is a delicious Peruvian nut-like grain. Combined with
a legume, such as lima beans, it is an great alternative to meat.
It is high in fiber and an excellent source of iron.*

Serves 4		
1 cup	quinoa	250 mL
1	package (12 oz/350 g) frozen lima beans	1
1 cup	thinly sliced carrots	250 mL
1 tbsp	vegetable oil	15 mL
	Salt and freshly ground black pepper	

1. Rinse quinoa under cold running water until water is clear. In a medium saucepan, bring quinoa and 1 cup (250 mL) water to a boil. Reduce heat. Cover and cook for 15 minutes or until tender. Drain and transfer to bowl.

2. In same saucepan, add a small amount of water to lima beans and carrots. Bring to a boil. Reduce heat and cook for 5 minutes or until vegetables are tender. Drain.

3. In a wok or frying pan, heat oil. Add quinoa, cooked vegetables and salt and pepper. Stir-fry until heated.

TOFU VEGETABLE QUICHE

Tofu does not have much flavor on its own, but it nicely takes on flavors of the foods with which it is prepared.

Serves 4

SEASONING TIP
Dried basil, oregano, tarragon, garlic powder or ground nutmeg are appropriate to use in this quiche.

- PREHEAT OVEN TO 350°F (180°C)
- 10-INCH (25 CM) QUICHE PAN OR DEEP PLATE, LIGHTLY GREASED

2 cups	coarsely chopped vegetables, such as bell pepper or zucchini	500 mL
½ cup	finely chopped onion	125 mL
2	eggs	2
1	package (19 oz/550 g) silken tofu, drained	1
	Salt and freshly ground black pepper	

1. In a large nonstick skillet, over medium-high heat, cook vegetables and onion for 10 minutes or until tender (add water if sticking occurs). Place in prepared pan.

2. In a food processor or blender, purée eggs and tofu until smooth and creamy. Add salt and pepper to taste. Pour tofu mixture over reserved vegetables.

3. Bake in preheated oven for 50 minutes or until knife inserted in the center comes out clean. Cut into 4 wedges and serve.

POLENTA WITH RED TOMATO SAUCE

Polenta, the comfort food staple of northern Italian cuisine, starts out as humble cornmeal. Excellent polenta is readily found in the deli counter of many supermarkets. It comes as a roll in a plastic sleeve. I suggest serving this simple tomato sauce version with steamed broccoli.

| | **Serves 4** |

• PREHEAT OVEN TO 350°F (180°C)
• OBLONG BAKING PAN, LINED WITH FOIL

½	roll (1 lb/500 g) prepared polenta (see Tip, left)	½
1 cup	Basic Red Tomato Sauce (see recipe, page 120) or store-bought	250 mL
¼ cup	freshly grated Parmesan cheese	50 mL
2 tsp	dried basil leaves or 2 tbsp (25 mL) chopped fresh	10 mL

TIP

An appetizer may be made from the remaining half roll of polenta. Thinly slice polenta and arrange on a baking sheet. Brush each slice with a little beaten egg, then sprinkle with grated Parmesan cheese. Bake in 400°F (200°C) oven for 15 minutes or until golden. Cut into quarters to serve.

1. Slice polenta into 8 pieces. Arrange in prepared pan. Evenly spread tomato sauce over polenta. Sprinkle with cheese and basil.

2. Bake in preheated oven for 12 minutes or until polenta and sauce are warm. Serve two slices per person.

BEAN TORTILLA PIE

Ever-popular flour tortillas stacked between a Mexican-inspired filling will bring back vacation memories. Tossed green salad and a dessert make this a pleasant lighter meal.

TIPS

Flour tortillas come as wraps in different colors and different flavors such as tomato, cheese, vegetable and so on.

Shredded cheese, which can be purchased in several types and sometimes, two or more types in the same package, saves preparation time.

- *PREHEAT OVEN TO 350°F (180°C)*
- *8-INCH (20 CM) ROUND PIE PLATE*

1	can (14 oz/398 mL) refried beans	1
1 tbsp	chili powder	15 mL
5	8-inch (20 cm) flour tortillas (see Tips, left)	5
1¼ cups	shredded cheese (see Tips, left)	300 mL

1. In a medium bowl, combine beans and chili powder.

2. Place 1 tortilla in prepared baking dish. Top with one-quarter bean mixture and ¼ cup (50 mL) cheese. Repeat layers three times ending with last tortilla. Sprinkle with remaining cheese.

3. Bake in preheated oven for 15 minutes or until cheese is melted and layers are heated through. Cut into 4 wedges to serve.

CORN CUSTARD

Serve these individual custards for a vegetarian lunch or as an accompaniment to dinner. In winter, make them with frozen corn but use fresh when it is available.

<table>
<tr><td rowspan="3">Makes 6</td><td colspan="3">• PREHEAT OVEN TO 350°F (180°C)</td></tr>
<tr><td colspan="3">• SIX (¾ CUP/175 ML) CUSTARD CUPS, WELL-GREASED</td></tr>
<tr><td colspan="3">• LARGE BAKING PAN</td></tr>
</table>

3 cups	corn kernels, divided	750 mL
2 cups	milk	500 mL
4	eggs	4
1	green onion, chopped or chopped fresh chives	1
	Salt and freshly ground black pepper	

1. In a large saucepan, simmer 2 cups (500 mL) corn kernels and milk for 20 minutes or until corn is tender. Remove from heat and cool.

2. In a food processor or blender, process corn mixture until smooth. Strain through a sieve, discarding solids. Whisk in eggs, onion, salt and pepper.

3. Divide remaining corn between custard cups. Add one-sixth of corn-egg mixture to each cup. Place cups in a large baking pan. Add enough hot water to pan to reach 1 inch (2.5 cm) up the sides of cups.

4. Bake in preheated oven for 30 minutes or until center is almost firm. Remove from oven. Cool for 5 minutes. Unmold from cups to serving plates.

SERVING SUGGESTION

- Accompany with sliced tomatoes with chopped fresh basil and a splash of balsamic vinegar. Add some crusty rolls.

VEGETABLES

SERVED ALONE OR WITH A DELICATE SAUCE OR TOPPING, VEGETABLES ARE an exciting part of each day's meals. Never before have so many vegetables been available virtually year-round. There was a time when they were called "the forgotten guest." No longer true. Everyone realizes the benefits of eating vegetables.

The secret of fine vegetable cookery is in the preparation, cooking times and temperatures and imaginative seasoning. Asian methods of preparing vegetables are the best — slightly underdone or tender-crisp. (For more information on cooking vegetables, see page 10.) Vegetables loose texture, flavor, color and nutrients when overcooked.

The Canadian and U.S. food guides suggest we eat numerous servings of vegetables each day because they are the best source of the antioxidant vitamins, the disease-preventing ones we hear so much about these days. As well, many vegetables are good sources of vitamins E and C, which along with beta-carotene, may play an important role in averting coronary artery disease. Vegetables, as well as fruit, are also a good source of fiber.

ROASTED GARLIC

Regarded as an appetizer, an addition to cooked vegetables or a soup ingredient, Roasted Garlic never fails to draw raves. What was a strong-juiced vegetable becomes through roasting, very mild and absolutely delicious. Whenever something this great is so easy, we wonder why we have not been doing it forever.

Makes about 1/4 cup (50 mL) paste

TIP
Roast more than one garlic head at a time. Freeze the extra for use another day.

• *PREHEAT OVEN TO 350°F (180°C)*

1	whole garlic head	1
	Olive oil	
	Salt and freshly ground black pepper	

1. Slice top of whole garlic head to expose some flesh on each garlic clove (about 1/4 inch/1 cm) off the top of garlic). Remove loose outer layers of skin on the exposed cloves.

2. Place on a baking pan and drizzle with olive oil. Season with salt and pepper.

3. Bake in preheated oven for about 30 minutes or until flesh is soft. Remove from oven and allow to cool.

4. Squeeze out the flesh holding the cooled head over a small bowl. The flesh can now be stirred into mashed potatoes, added to melted butter or margarine or spooned directly into bubbling soup or over cooked vegetables. The added flavor is quite magical.

SIMPLE VEGGIE MARINADE

This very simple and classic marinade is a wonderful one that you can use for fresh or cooked vegetables.

Makes about 1/3 cup (75 mL)

1/4 cup	freshly squeezed lemon juice	50 mL
3 tbsp	canola oil	45 mL
2	cloves garlic, minced	2
2 tbsp	chopped fresh oregano leaves or 2 tsp (10 mL) dried	25 mL
	Salt and freshly ground black pepper	

1. In a tightly covered container, combine lemon juice, oil, garlic, oregano, salt and pepper. Shake until well blended. Store in the refrigerator until needed for up to one week.

SERVING SUGGESTIONS

- Toss cherry tomatoes, zucchini, green or red bell pepper chunks, eggplant, mushrooms and onions with marinade. Or brush it on vegetables grilling on the barbecue.

SAUTÉED SKILLET PEPPERS

One day, while cleaning out the refrigerator, I found lurking in its nether regions several bell peppers of different colors. They were still fresh but needed to be used before becoming otherwise. Thus inspired, I developed the following recipe that I found absolutely delicious served on toast for lunch.

Serves 4	1	each green, red and yellow bell pepper	1
	2 tsp	olive oil	10 mL
	1	clove garlic, sliced	1
		Salt and freshly ground black pepper	
	2 tbsp	freshly grated Parmesan cheese	25 mL

1. Remove and discard seeds from peppers. Cut peppers into long strips.

2. In a nonstick skillet, heat oil over medium heat. Add garlic and cook for 30 seconds. Add pepper slices. Reduce heat to medium-low. Cover and cook for 15 minutes or until peppers are tender and no longer moist, stirring occasionally. Season lightly with salt and pepper.

3. Sprinkle with cheese. Cover and cook on low for 5 minutes or until cheese is melted.

GRILLED VEGETABLES

Vegetables such as onion, garlic and bell pepper contain natural sugars that caramelize when grilled, giving a depth of flavor that pan sautéing could never match.

	Serves 4	

TIP

Using a grill basket keeps vegetable pieces from falling onto the burner. But if you like the grill marks, by all means place vegetables directly on the grills. Just make sure grills are clean so vegetables do not absorb flavors of other meals. It is best to cook with the barbecue lid down, using direct heat, directly over the hot fire.

• PREHEAT BARBECUE

2	large bell peppers, any color, halved and seeded	2
1	eggplant, cut lengthwise into thin slices	1
	Olive oil	
	Salt and freshly ground black pepper	

1. Brush pepper halves and eggplant slices lightly with olive oil.

2. On a rack or in a basket (see Tip, left), grill pepper halves over medium-high heat for 20 minutes or until skin is blackened. Remove peppers to a paper or plastic bag until cool. Peel away blackened skin and cut into smaller pieces.

3. Grill sliced eggplant over medium-high heat, turning once, for 4 minutes per side or until flesh is tender. Season lightly with salt and pepper.

SKILLET-STYLE ONION AND SWEET POTATOES

Eye appeal and great taste make this vegetable dish a pleasing addition to the dinner plate. Vitamin C and beta-carotene make it very nutritious. And it can be prepared in very short order!

	Serves 4	

1 tbsp	olive oil	15 mL
1	large onion, sliced	1
2	large sweet potatoes, peeled and thinly sliced (see Nutrition Tip, page 149)	2
2/3 cup	vegetable stock	150 mL
	Salt and freshly ground black pepper	

1. In a nonstick skillet, heat oil over medium heat. Cook onion, stirring frequently, for 5 minutes or until soft.

2. Add potatoes and stock. Cover and bring to a boil. Reduce heat to medium-low and cook slowly, stirring frequently, for 15 minutes or until potatoes are tender. Season lightly with salt and pepper.

CRÈME FRAÎCHE MASHED POTATOES

Delicate in flavor, these mashed potatoes are most suited to poultry. Serve them at once or cover and refrigerate for up to 2 days and then reheat (see Tip, left). They also freeze well.

Serves 4

TIP
Reheat refrigerated potatoes in a covered baking dish in a 300°F (150°C) oven for 30 minutes or until hot.

4	medium Yukon Gold potatoes or any other good mashing potato, peeled and cut into chunks	4
½ cup	crème fraîche (see recipe, below) or sour cream	125 mL
2 tbsp	butter or margarine	25 mL
¼ tsp	ground nutmeg	1 mL
	Salt and freshly ground black pepper	

1. In a medium saucepan, cook potatoes in boiling water for 20 minutes or until just tender. Drain and return to saucepan. Then mash potatoes.

2. Add crème fraîche and butter. Beat with a potato masher until potatoes are smooth and fluffy. Stir in nutmeg and salt and pepper to taste.

CRÈME FRAÎCHE
- In a glass container, combine 1 cup (250 mL) whipping (35%) cream and 2 tbsp (25 mL) buttermilk. Cover and let stand at room temperature from 8 to 24 hours or until very thick. Stir well before refrigerating. It keeps for up to 10 days.

HORSERADISH MASHED POTATOES

Horseradish makes these mashed potatoes especially suited for beef or pork. Serve them at once or cover and refrigerate for up to 2 days and then reheat (see Tips, left). They also freeze well.

Serves 4

TIPS
Reheat refrigerated potatoes in a covered baking dish in a 300°F (150°C) oven for 30 minutes or until hot.

The Prince Edward Island Potato Board does not recommend using an electric mixer because it makes the potatoes "gluey." It is their number one telephone complaint.

4	medium Yukon Gold potatoes or any other good mashing potato, peeled and cut into chunks	4
½ cup	sour cream	125 mL
2 tbsp	horseradish	25 mL
1	green onion, thinly sliced	1
	Salt and freshly ground black pepper	

1. In a medium saucepan, cook potatoes in boiling water for 20 minutes or until just tender. Drain and return to saucepan. Then mash potatoes.

2. Add sour cream and horseradish. Beat with a potato masher until potatoes are smooth and fluffy (see Tips, left). Stir in onions and salt and pepper to taste.

FABULOUS FRENCH FRIES

Easy as opening a package of potatoes and twice as good! Great served with grilled steak or pork chops and a salad.

Serves 4

• PREHEAT OVEN TO 400°F (200°C)
• RIMMED BAKING SHEET, LIGHTLY GREASED

1	package (2 lbs/1 kg) shoestring French fry potatoes	1
2	cloves garlic, minced	2
	Zest of 1 lemon	
	Salt and freshly ground black pepper	

1. Place potatoes in a large bowl. Toss with garlic, lemon zest and a dash of salt and pepper.

2. Spread on prepared baking sheet. Bake in preheated oven according to package directions. Turn potatoes occasionally to brown evenly.

SWEET POTATO FRENCH FRIES

The ease of making French fries the oven way! This time, we do it with sweet potatoes, which cook even faster than the white varieties.

Serves 4		

NUTRITION TIP

Foods rich in beta-carotene are the dark orange and red vegetables and fruits such as sweet potatoes and carrots, as well as pink grapefruit.

Because of the rich flavor in sweet potatoes, they have earned a bad reputation of being high in calories. In reality, a 5-inch (12.5 cm) sweet potato contains only about 120 calories — no more than a white one of the same size.

- PREHEAT OVEN TO 425°F (220°C)
- RIMMED BAKING SHEET, LIGHTLY GREASED

2	medium sweet potatoes, peeled	2
2 tbsp	olive oil	25 mL
2	cloves garlic, finely chopped	2
½ tsp	dried tarragon or 2 tsp (10 mL) chopped fresh	2 mL
	Salt and freshly ground black pepper	

1. Cut each potato into ½-inch (1 cm) thick slices. Cut each slice lengthwise into ½-inch (1 cm) strips. Place in a shallow bowl or plastic bag.

2. Add oil, garlic, tarragon and a dash of salt and pepper. Toss until coated.

3. Spread on prepared baking sheet. Bake in preheated oven for 15 minutes or until potatoes are tender, turning once.

SCALLOPED POTATOES WITH MUSHROOMS

Mushrooms add wonderful flavor and moisture to this traditional potato dish.

Serves 4

NUTRITION TIP
For bone-building calcium, top potatoes with cheese.

TIPS
This recipe is easily doubled but needs about 15 minutes extra baking time.

Use any mushrooms providing they measure 1½ cups (375 mL).

• PREHEAT OVEN TO 350°F (180°C)
• DEEP 6-CUP (1.5 L) BAKING DISH, GREASED

3 cups	sliced potatoes (about 3 medium)	750 mL
1½ cups	sliced white mushrooms (6 medium)	375 mL
	Salt and freshly ground black pepper	
½ cup	chicken or vegetable stock	125 mL
2 tbsp	butter or margarine	25 mL

1. Arrange half the potatoes in prepared dish. Top with mushrooms. Sprinkle each layer lightly with salt and pepper. Add remaining potatoes.

2. Heat stock with butter. Pour over vegetables. Cover and bake in preheated oven for 30 minutes. Uncover and bake for 20 minutes more or until potatoes are tender and golden brown. Remove from oven. Let stand for 10 minutes before serving.

MUSHROOM NOTES

• Buy mushrooms that are firm, evenly colored with tightly closed caps. If the underneath gills are visible, the mushroom is past its prime. Buy them of a similar size so they cook evenly.

• Store in a single layer on a tray in the refrigerator, covered with damp paper towel for no longer than three days.

• Do not clean until just before use. Either brush with a soft brush or wipe with a damp paper towel to remove dirt.

• Never soak mushrooms as they will absorb water and turn mushy.

• Trim a thin slice off the stem before using.

• When sautéing, be sure the pan and oil are hot. Mushrooms give off a lot of liquid. Stir and cook until all liquid evaporates.

SCALLOPED POTATOES WITH CHEESE

A French import, this recipe is sometimes known as Gratin Dauphinois. Easy and satisfying, this sophisticated version of scalloped potatoes is great served with roasted, grilled or broiled meats. The recipe has lots of versatility since you can make it with just about any cheese and any type of potato, including sweet.

Serves 6

TIP
For a less rich version, use chicken or vegetable stock instead of the milk.

• *PREHEAT OVEN TO 425°F (220°C)*
• *11-BY 7-INCH (2 L) BAKING DISH, GREASED*

6	small red-skinned potatoes, cut into thick slices, divided	6
2 tbsp	butter or margarine, melted, divided	25 mL
½ cup	shredded Gruyère cheese, divided	125 mL
	Salt and freshly ground black pepper	
1 cup	milk (see Tip, left)	250 mL

1. Arrange half the potatoes in prepared dish. Drizzle with half the butter. Top with half the cheese and season lightly with salt and pepper. Repeat layers.

2. Heat milk. Pour over potato mixture. Bake in preheated oven, uncovered, for 40 minutes or until potatoes are tender and golden brown.

POTATOES AND THE "OTHER ROOTS"

- In addition to potatoes, the other root vegetables include carrots, beets, parsnips, rutabagas and turnips.
- If a potato has a greenish hue below the skin, it has had too much exposure to bright light. You don't have to throw away the entire potato, just cut away and discard any green portions. Always store potatoes away from sunlight. Refrigeration is not recommended; however, the other root vegetables do store best in the refrigerator.

POTATOES ANNA

Potatoes Anna is everything a great vegetable recipe should be! It's beautiful to look at, easy to make and has a wonderfully dressed-up taste.

Serves 6		

- *PREHEAT OVEN TO 450°F (230°C)*
- *HEAVY OVENPROOF SKILLET*

¼ cup	melted butter or margarine, divided	50 mL
2 lbs	baking potatoes, peeled and sliced very thin	1 kg
1 tsp	coarse salt	5 mL
½ tsp	freshly ground black pepper	2 mL
	Freshly chopped parsley	

1. Drizzle 2 tbsp (25 mL) butter in skillet. Place a single layer of potatoes, slightly overlapping, in a circular pattern in pan. Sprinkle with ¼ tsp (1 mL) salt and a little pepper.

2. Repeat layers, drizzling ½ tsp (2 mL) butter over each layer until all potato is used, ending with butter. Press firmly with back of spoon to flatten. Cover and bake in preheated oven for 45 minutes.

3. Uncover and bake 20 minutes more or until potatoes are tender and golden brown. Turn out onto plate. Sprinkle with parsley.

CARROT RUTABAGA PURÉE

This vegetable combination tastes so wonderful, you'll want to make enough extra to freeze. Rutabagas are a good source of vitamin C.

Serves 6 to 8		

TIP
Store the purée in the refrigerator for up to 3 days or freeze for longer storage.

2	medium rutabagas, peeled and cut into cubes	2
5	medium carrots, peeled and cut into pieces	5
3 tbsp	butter or margarine	45 mL
3 tbsp	packed light brown sugar	45 mL
	Salt and freshly ground black pepper	

TIP
Rutabaga has a thin, pale yellow skin and a slightly sweet, firm flesh of the same color. It is available year-round.

1. In a large saucepan, cook rutabaga and carrots in boiling water for 30 minutes or until vegetables are tender. Drain well.

2. Transfer vegetables to a food processor. Add butter and sugar. Pulse with on/off motions until smooth. Return to saucepan. Season lightly with salt and pepper. Reheat to serving temperature.

MINTED-CHIVE NEW POTATOES

Scrubbed red and white new potatoes, cooked in boiling water until tender and served with butter sauce, must be one of the great delights of early summer.

Serves 8

TIP
Place an apple in the potato bag, to avoid sprouting.

¼ cup	chopped fresh mint	50 mL
2 tbsp	chopped fresh chives	25 mL
⅓ cup	melted butter or margarine	75 mL
4	each small red and white new potatoes, scrubbed	4
	Salt and freshly ground black pepper	
	Light sour cream or plain yogurt, optional	

1. In a small container, combine mint, chives and butter. Set aside.

2. In a medium saucepan, cook potatoes in boiling water for 15 minutes or until tender. Drain well.

3. Toss cooked potatoes with butter mixture. Add salt and a generous sprinkle of freshly ground pepper.

4. At the table pass sour cream or yogurt, if using.

SCALLOPED VEGETABLE CASSEROLE

This casserole is easy and can be adapted for various vegetables. You may use onions, squash, cauliflower or mushrooms to substitute for the broccoli and/or the potatoes. Your choice depends on the entrée you are serving with them.

Serves 4		

TIP
Finely grated Parmesan cheese makes a nice change.

• *PREHEAT OVEN TO 400°F (200°C)*
• *6-CUP (1.5 L) CASSEROLE DISH, GREASED*

3 cups	thinly sliced potatoes (about 3 medium)	750 mL
2 cups	chopped broccoli, florets and stem	500 mL
½ cup	Tomato French Dressing (see recipe, page 64) or store-bought	125 mL
½ cup	shredded Cheddar cheese (see Tip, left)	125 mL
	Salt and freshly ground black pepper	

1. Layer potatoes and broccoli in prepared casserole.

2. In a small bowl, combine ½ cup (125 mL) water, dressing and cheese. Pour mixture over vegetables. Season lightly with salt and pepper.

3. Cover and bake in preheated oven for 45 minutes or until vegetables are tender and cheese is melted.

ORIENTAL BROCCOLI

Broccoli is one of the most readily available fresh green vegetables during the winter, making it a natural winter side dish for northern dwellers. And it is frequently one of the most reasonably priced.

Serves 4		

1	bunch broccoli	1
1	small red bell pepper	1
1 tbsp	butter or margarine	15 mL
3 tbsp	teriyaki sauce	45 mL
	Freshly ground black pepper	

1. Trim broccoli and cut into florets. Set aside.

2. Cut red pepper in half, core and seed. Cut into thin slices. In a shallow saucepan, melt butter over medium heat. Add peppers. Stir-fry for 2 minutes or until peppers start to soften.

3. Add teriyaki and broccoli to pan, stirring to coat thoroughly. Add ¼ cup (50 mL) water. Cover and cook, stirring occasionally, for 5 minutes or until broccoli is tender-crisp.

4. Using a slotted spoon, transfer peppers and broccoli to a warm serving dish. Season lightly with pepper.

5. Boil remaining liquid briefly to form a glaze. Pour over vegetables and serve.

BROILED PLUM TOMATOES

Summer, when the tomatoes are at their plentiful best, is the perfect time to serve this wonderful vegetable treat. Cook only for a very short time and serve them warm.

Serves 6

TIP
You can replace the mozzarella with grated Parmesan. It provides a crispy and golden brown topping. A dusting of dried basil is also nice.

• *PREHEAT BROILER*

6	large plum tomatoes, halved lengthwise	6
1 tbsp	olive oil	15 mL
⅓ cup	seasoned dry bread crumbs	75 mL
¼ cup	shredded mozzarella cheese (see Tip, left)	50 mL
	Salt and freshly ground black pepper	

1. Scoop out some of the tomato seeds and discard. Place tomatoes on broiler pan. Drizzle evenly with olive oil.

2. Combine bread crumbs and cheese. Spoon evenly over each tomato half. Season lightly with salt and pepper.

3. Broil for 2 minutes or until warm, cheese melts and bread crumbs are toasted.

SWEDISH RUTABAGA

*Our family has always been fond of rutabaga (still called turnip by many).
It is the root vegetable with a pale yellow skin and a slightly sweet, firm
yellow flesh of the same color. This version adds sour cream and nutmeg to
the cooked vegetable. The result is a very mild and tasty side dish
that goes particularly well with pork and poultry.*

Serves 4			
1	medium rutabaga, peeled and cut into pieces	1
¼ cup	sour cream	50 mL
2 tbsp	butter or margarine	25 mL
½ tsp	ground nutmeg	2 mL
	Salt and freshly ground black pepper	
	Granulated sugar, optional	

1. In a medium saucepan, cook rutabaga in boiling water for 15 minutes or until tender. Remove from heat. Drain well and return to saucepan.

2. Mash rutabaga with a potato masher. Mash in sour cream and butter until smooth. Stir in nutmeg and season lightly with salt and pepper. Taste and add a small amount of sugar, if extra sweetness is desired.

MAPLE-GLAZED CARROTS

*You'll be amazed at the classy taste the maple syrup gives
the humble carrot. Add to this the elusive smoky flavor of bacon.*

Serves 4			
1 lb	carrots, peeled and cut lengthwise	500 g
3	slices bacon, chopped	3
1	medium apple, peeled and cored	1
2 tbsp	pure maple syrup	25 mL
	Salt and freshly ground black pepper	

1. In a saucepan, cook carrots in boiling water for 10 minutes or until tender-crisp. Drain.

2. In a nonstick skillet, cook bacon on medium heat for 3 minutes or until lightly browned.

3. Slice apple into thin wedges. Add to bacon and cook for 2 minutes.

4. Add carrots, maple syrup, salt and pepper. Stir frequently until carrots are warmed through and lightly glazed. Serve immediately.

WINE-GLAZED VEGETABLES

Root vegetables with bold flavors are best for this recipe. A sweet wine complements them. Rutabaga and carrots are called for here, but turnip, parsnips and beets can be substituted for either.

Serves 4

Variation
Sherry, port or another dessert wine are all suitable substitutes for the sweet white wine.

• *LARGE HEAVY SAUCEPAN OR DUTCH OVEN*

I	medium rutabaga, peeled and diced	I
2	medium carrots, peeled and sliced	2
½ cup	sweet white wine (see Variation, left)	125 mL
2 tbsp	butter or margarine	25 mL
	Salt and freshly ground black pepper	

1. In a saucepan, combine rutabaga, carrots and 2 cups (500 mL) water. Bring to a boil. Cover and reduce heat to medium-low. Cook for 15 minutes or until vegetables are tender.

2. Drain well. Return to saucepan. Add wine and butter. Cook over high heat, stirring occasionally, for 5 minutes or until all liquid is evaporated. Season lightly with salt and pepper.

ROASTED ASPARAGUS

Toss veggies with enough oil to lightly coat so they don't dry out during roasting. With asparagus, a newcomer on the roasting block, this is especially appropriate. Choose asparagus carefully, by selecting firm, vivid green stalks with tightly closed tips and cook them as soon as possible.

Serves 6

Tomato Variation
Grape or cherry tomatoes may be treated in the same way as the asparagus. Cut tomatoes in half and toss in oil and vinegar mixture. Roast for 30 minutes or until tomatoes are shriveled. Or you can do a combination of the asparagus and tomatoes, but cook tomatoes for 15 minutes first, then add asparagus and cook an additional 20 minutes or until asparagus is tender.

* *PREHEAT OVEN TO 450°F (230°C)*
* *BAKING DISH, GREASED*

I lb	asparagus	500 g
I	clove garlic, minced	I
I tbsp	olive oil	15 mL
I tbsp	balsamic vinegar	15 mL
	Salt and freshly ground black pepper	

1. Break asparagus stalks at natural breaking point. Toss with garlic, oil, vinegar, salt and pepper. Place in prepared baking dish.

2. Roast in preheated oven, uncovered, turning once, for 20 minutes or until asparagus is tender.

ONION-ROASTED ASPARAGUS

Since asparagus roasts so well, I tried this version, adding the flavor of onions.

Serves 4 to 6

* *PREHEAT OVEN TO 450°F (230°C)*
* *BAKING DISH, GREASED*

I ½ lbs	asparagus	750 g
2 tbsp	butter or margarine	25 mL
½	package (1.5 oz/45 g) onion soup mix	½
	Freshly ground black pepper	

1. Break asparagus stalks at natural breaking point. Place in prepared baking dish.

2. Melt butter. Stir in soup mix. Drizzle mixture over asparagus. Sprinkle lightly with pepper.

3. Cover and bake in preheated oven for 20 minutes or until asparagus is tender-crisp.

ASPARAGUS TERIYAKI

- Drizzle teriyaki sauce over asparagus before baking.

ROASTED BEETS WITH CARROTS

Substantial vegetables with a lot of flavor and fiber, such as beets and carrots, are the best candidates for roasting. Although the roasting of the two vegetables takes a little over an hour, the end results are simply superb. In fact, the beets can be completed up to 2 days ahead, chilled and finished just before serving.

Serves 4

Variation
Roasted Cauliflower
Replace beets and carrots with 1 large cauliflower, broken into small florets. Combine oil, 1 tsp (5 mL) chopped fresh rosemary, salt and pepper. Toss with cauliflower to coat. Place in a single layer on a greased baking dish. Bake in a 400°F (200°C) preheated oven for 25 minutes or until cooked through and lightly browned.

- PREHEAT OVEN TO 425°F (220°C)
- BAKING DISH, GREASED

3	medium beets, trimmed	3
3	medium carrots, peeled and cut diagonally into ¾-inch (2 cm) slices	3
2 tbsp	olive oil	25 mL
	Salt and freshly ground black pepper	

1. Wrap beets tightly with foil into one large package. Roast for 1¼ hours or until beets are tender.

2. Meanwhile, toss carrots with oil, salt and pepper. Place in a shallow baking dish and roast in preheated oven for 20 minutes or until almost tender. Remove vegetables from oven.

3. When beets are cool enough to handle, open foil and remove skin. Cut each into 8 wedges.

4. Add beets to carrots and toss to combine. Roast for 15 minutes more or until beets are hot and carrots are very tender.

ROASTED BUTTERNUT SQUASH

The wonderful aroma of baking squash is so appealing. Try roasting it with some olive oil. The aromas are even better. So is the taste!

Serves 4

TIP
Tossing ingredients of an oily nature in a clean plastic bag makes for short and easy clean up. If your milk comes in heavy individual bags, cut one end of an emptied bag, wash and reuse for this purpose.

• *PREHEAT OVEN TO 400°F (200°C)*
• *BAKING PAN, LINED WITH FOIL*

I	medium butternut squash, peeled	I
I to 2 tsp	minced fresh gingerroot	5 to 10 mL
I	large clove garlic, minced	I
I tbsp	olive oil	15 mL
	Salt and freshly ground black pepper	

1. Cut squash into bite-size cubes.
2. In a large bowl or plastic bag (see Tip, left), toss squash, gingerroot, garlic, oil, salt and pepper.
3. Arrange on prepared baking pan in a single layer. Bake in preheated oven, stirring occasionally, for 40 minutes or until tender and starting to brown.

SAUTÉ OF SPRING VEGETABLES

Served with either salmon or lamb, this is a perfect accompaniment for a great spring-into-summer dinner.

Serves 6

TIP
Add chopped fresh mint for a special springtime flavor. About 2 tbsp (25 mL) chopped should be enough.

I lb	asparagus	500 g
I lb	snow peas	500 g
I lb	baby carrots	500 g
2 tbsp	butter or margarine	25 mL
	Salt and freshly ground black pepper	

1. Break asparagus stalks at natural breaking point. Cut asparagus into 1-inch (2.5 cm) pieces. Trim snow peas.

recipe continues on page 161

Maple-Glazed Baked Peaches *(page 167)* ▶

2. In a medium saucepan, bring water to a boil. Steam asparagus in a steamer basket for 1 minute. Remove basket and refresh under cold running water. Add snow peas to basket. Steam for 30 seconds. Remove basket and refresh under cold running water. Repeat with carrots. Steam for 5 minutes. Spread all vegetables on paper towels to dry.

3. In a nonstick skillet, melt butter over medium-high heat. Add asparagus, snow peas, carrots and salt and pepper. Cook for about 4 minutes.

CARAMELIZED VIDALIA ONIONS

Anytime Vidalia onions are in your supermarket, remember to make this wonderful side dish. Named for Vidalia, Georgia, where they are grown, these large, pale yellow onions are exceedingly sweet and juicy.

Serves 4		
1	large Vidalia onion (see Tip, left)	1
2 tbsp	olive oil	25 mL
1 tbsp	packed brown sugar	15 mL
1 tbsp	balsamic vinegar	15 mL
	Salt and freshly ground black pepper	

TIP
When Vidalia onions are unavailable, replace them with any sweet mild onion such as a Bermuda or Spanish onion.

1. Peel and cut onion in half. Slice each half into thin slices (you will have about 4 cups/1 L).

2. In a large nonstick skillet, heat oil over low heat. Add onion and sugar. Cook, uncovered, stirring frequently, for 25 minutes or until onion is very tender and beginning to caramelize.

3. Stir in vinegar. Season lightly with salt and pepper.

SERVING SUGGESTIONS
- This onion dish is wonderful served warm with grilled steak, pork chops, burgers or grilled lamb. I also enjoy a serving with boiled perogies topped with a small spoonful of sour cream.

◄ Summer Fruit Parfait *(page 174)*

BAKED SUMMER VEGETABLE LAYERS

Typical Italian flavors are blended in this tasty side dish. I make it with a sprinkling of the popular herbs, oregano and basil.

<table>
<tr><td colspan="3">

Serves 4

</td></tr>
</table>

• PREHEAT OVEN TO 425°F (220°C)
• 8-INCH (2 L) SHALLOW BAKING DISH, GREASED

4	medium potatoes, peeled and thinly sliced, divided	4
I	onion, thinly sliced	I
I	small zucchini, thinly sliced	I
	Chopped fresh oregano or basil leaves, optional	
	Salt and freshly ground black pepper	
2	tomatoes, sliced	2

1. In prepared baking dish, arrange half the potatoes in an even layer. Spread onion and then zucchini on top. Sprinkle evenly with half of oregano and basil, if using, salt and pepper.

2. Repeat with remaining potatoes and top with tomato slices. Sprinkle evenly with herbs again. Add 1/4 cup (50 mL) water.

3. Cover and bake in preheated oven for 20 minutes. Uncover and bake for 20 minutes more or until potatoes are tender.

BAKED WINTER VEGETABLE LAYERS

Root-type vegetables are particularly appropriate for this recipe since they all require approximately the same cooking time. For a change, use parsnips, red onions and thinly sliced carrots.

Serves 4

• PREHEAT OVEN TO 375°F (190°C)
• 9-INCH (23 CM) DEEP PIE PLATE, GREASED

1 tbsp	butter or margarine	15 mL
6	green onions, sliced	6
2	large potatoes, sliced	2
1	large beet, peeled and sliced	1
	Salt and freshly ground black pepper	

1. In a nonstick skillet, melt butter on medium heat. Add onions and cook, stirring, for 5 minutes or until tender.

2. In pie plate, layer potato, half of cooked onions, beet and more onions in pie plate. Sprinkle each layer lightly with salt and pepper. Add a small amount of water.

3. Cover and bake in preheated oven for about 1 hour or until vegetables are tender.

ROASTED ROOT VEGETABLES

Root vegetables may be roasted individually or in combinations. Since most root vegetables take about the same amount of time to cook, timing is not a problem, just cut them into similar size pieces. Root vegetable choices include parsnips, turnip, rutabaga, red, white or sweet potatoes, carrots, onions and beets.

Serves 4	

• PREHEAT OVEN TO 450°F (230°C)
• LARGE RIMMED BAKING SHEET

I lb	root vegetables (see Intro, above)	500 g
2 tbsp	vegetable or olive oil	25 mL
I to 2	cloves garlic, minced	I to 2
	Salt and freshly ground black pepper	

1. Peel and cut vegetables into bite-size chunks. In a large bowl or plastic bag (see Tip, page 80), toss vegetables with oil and garlic. Lightly season with salt and pepper. Arrange on baking sheet in a single layer.

2. Roast in preheated oven, turning partway through, for 30 minutes or until tender and golden brown.

LEMON-HERB SNOW PEAS

A simply delicious way to dress up snow peas.

Serves 4	

I tbsp	butter or margarine, melted	15 mL
I tsp	freshly grated lemon zest	5 mL
½ tsp	dried tarragon or I tbsp (15 mL) fresh	2 mL
I lb	snow peas, trimmed	500 g
	Salt and freshly ground black pepper	

1. In a small dish, combine butter, lemon zest and tarragon. Set aside.

2. In a large saucepan, cook snow peas in boiling water for 2 minutes or until tender-crisp. Drain well. Transfer to a warm serving bowl. Add butter mixture and toss to coat. Season lightly with salt and pepper.

DESSERTS & DESSERT SAUCES

I LOVE THE EXPRESSION "LIFE IS SHORT, EAT DESSERT FIRST." I AM NOT alone. My husband's usual dinner time question is "And what's for D?" This may be why I have more recipes in the dessert chapter than in any other.

I discuss fruit in this chapter because it plays such an important role in many desserts, just as it plays an important role in most of our meals. We serve fruit throughout the day from breakfast to dinner dessert.

RASPBERRY MOUSSE

Light and luscious best describes this dessert. You can make it with fresh fruit throughout most of the summer by substituting strawberries and then peaches for equally delicious results.

Serves 6		

2 cups	fresh or frozen raspberries, thawed if frozen	500 mL
⅓ cup	granulated sugar	75 mL
I	envelope (¼ oz/7 g) unflavored gelatin	I
I cup	whipping (35%) cream	250 mL
	Raspberries for garnish, optional	

1. Press raspberries through a fine mesh sieve into a large bowl. Discard seeds. Stir in sugar.

2. In a small saucepan, sprinkle gelatin in 2 tbsp (25 mL) water. Let stand for 5 minutes or until softened. Heat on very low, stirring frequently, until gelatin is dissolved. Stir into raspberry mixture. Refrigerate until partly set.

3. Meanwhile, whip cream until stiff peaks form. Fold into raspberry mixture. Spoon into six dessert dishes. Serve garnished with extra raspberries, if desired.

CITRUS-BAKED APPLE SLICES

Slow baking transforms thick apple slices into a rich and luscious dessert for dinner or an elegant breakfast. The result, wonderful golden apple slices with an appealing hint of lemon, is worth the extra time. Serve them alone, with a spice cake or over pancakes or waffles.

Makes 4 cups (1 L)		

• PREHEAT OVEN TO 300°F (150°C)
• 13-BY 9-INCH (3 L) GLASS BAKING DISH, UNGREASED

½ cup	liquid honey (see Tips, above right)	125 mL
	Juice and zest of ½ a lemon	
Pinch	ground nutmeg	Pinch
8 cups	thick slices peeled tart apples, about 6 large (see Tips, above right)	2 L

For a different flavor, replace honey with a strong maple syrup as the sweetener.

Apple varieties such as Empire, Cortland or Northern Spy are good choices here. If you are using a firm apple, such as a Spy, the apple slices will remain intact but soft.

1. In a large bowl, combine honey, $\frac{1}{3}$ cup (75 mL) water, lemon juice and zest. Add apple slices, stirring to coat well.

2. Place apples and liquid in a single layer in dish. Cover with foil and bake in preheated oven for 45 minutes or until apples are soft. Remove foil. Bake for about 75 minutes more or until apples are golden and most of the liquid has evaporated. Using a large spoon, gently turn slices once or twice during baking to keep them moist.

3. Pack into clean jars or plastic containers to within $\frac{1}{2}$ inch (1 cm) of rim. Cover with tight-fitting lids. Store in refrigerator for up to 3 weeks or freeze for longer storage.

MAPLE-GLAZED BAKED PEACHES

Maple-flavored peaches with a hint of ginger are a grand end to any dinner. A scoop of ice cream adds a nice finish.

Serves 4

TIP
When using peaches you'll want to peel them. First cut a shallow "x" in bottom. Then plunge into boiling water for 15 seconds. Transfer to ice water and the peeling is easy.

Variation
You can replace the peaches with pears.

• PREHEAT OVEN TO 400°F (200°C)
• 8-INCH (2 L) SQUARE BAKING DISH, UNGREASED

4	large peaches	4
$\frac{1}{3}$ cup	pure maple syrup	75 mL
$\frac{1}{3}$ cup	whipping (35%) cream	75 mL
2 tbsp	finely chopped candied ginger	25 mL

1. Peel peaches. Cut into thick slices and place in baking dish.

2. Stir together maple syrup and whipping cream. Drizzle over peaches. Sprinkle with ginger.

3. Bake in preheated oven for 20 minutes or until peaches are tender and glazed with sauce.

SAUTÉED PEARS

A scoop of ice cream and crisp gingersnap cookies
add a special touch to this simple dessert.

Serves 4			
2 cups	sliced pears (about 2)	500 mL
1 tsp	freshly squeezed lemon juice	5 mL
1 tbsp	butter or margarine	15 mL
2 tbsp	packed brown sugar	25 mL

Variation
You can substitute apples, wedges of fresh pineapple or firm peaches for the pears.

1. Toss pears with lemon juice.

2. In a nonstick skillet, heat butter on medium-high heat. Add pears. Sauté for 5 minutes or until tender.

3. Stir in brown sugar. Heat until sugar is melted. Serve warm.

FRUIT KEBABS WITH FRUIT YOGURT

Either grill the fruit kebabs or serve them fresh and uncooked.
Any flavor of fruit yogurt works well, although I prefer lemon or orange.

Serves 4			
• WOODEN SKEWERS			
12 to 16	large pieces of fresh fruit such as pineapple, mango, banana, peaches, whole strawberries or a combination of these	12 to 16
1 cup	plain yogurt	250 mL
¼ cup	frozen orange juice concentrate, thawed	50 mL
1 tbsp	liquid honey	15 mL

Variation
Lemon-flavored Yogurt
Replace the orange juice with 1 tsp (5 mL) grated lemon zest and 1 tbsp (15 mL) lemon juice plus a small amount of sugar.

1. Thread fruit onto wooden skewers. If using more than one kind of fruit, alternate for an attractive appearance.

2. In a small bowl, whisk together yogurt, orange juice and honey.

3. If cooking the kebabs, grill for 4 minutes per side over preheated medium-high barbecue until hot. Serve immediately with the yogurt mixture.

MERINGUE-TOPPED GRAPEFRUIT

Pink grapefruit is most attractive in this easy winter dessert.

Serves 4	• PREHEAT OVEN TO 425°F (220°C)	
2	large pink grapefruits, halved	2
2 tbsp	packed light brown sugar	25 mL
4	egg whites	4
Pinch	salt	Pinch
1/3 cup	granulated sugar	75 mL

1. Discard seeds from grapefruit. Cut segments free from membrane without removing them.

2. Place grapefruit halves on a baking pan. Sprinkle tops evenly with brown sugar.

3. In a medium bowl, with an electric mixer, beat egg whites with salt until soft peaks form. Gradually beat in granulated sugar until meringue is stiff and glossy.

4. Spoon a generous amount of meringue over each grapefruit half. Bake in preheated oven for 6 minutes or until meringue is golden. Serve at once.

ORANGES WITH ROSEMARY HONEY

This easy-to-make aromatic dessert is a welcome end to a heavier meal.

Serves 4		

TIP
Choose firm, heavy seedless oranges. Blood oranges make a great presentation. They are bright red with a sweet-tart flavor. Sadly, they are only available for a few months in the winter.

4	oranges (see Tip, left)	4
3 tbsp	liquid honey	45 mL
I tsp	finely chopped fresh rosemary or ½ tsp (2 mL) dried	5 mL

1. Remove peel and white pith from oranges. Cut each orange into crosswise slices ¼ inch (0.5 cm) thick. Arrange on a serving plate.

2. Meanwhile, in a small saucepan, bring honey, 2 tbsp (25 mL) water and rosemary to a simmer. Remove from heat. Cover and let steep for 15 minutes.

3. Pour honey liquid through a sieve to remove herb particles. Drizzle over orange slices.

GINGER RICOTTA CREAM

Keep a container of this creamy ricotta in the refrigerator year-round. Use it with fresh or canned fruit, such as halved pears or peaches, apples or nectarines, pineapple spears or whole strawberries.

Makes 2 cups (500 mL)		

2 cups	smooth ricotta cheese	500 mL
¼ cup	confectioner's (icing) sugar	50 mL
3 tbsp	finely chopped crystallized ginger	45 mL
I tsp	freshly grated lemon zest	5 mL

1. In a large bowl, with an electric mixer, beat cheese and sugar until smooth. Stir in ginger and lemon zest. Serve at once or store in a tightly sealed container in the refrigerator for up to 2 weeks.

FRUIT DIP

If you are inspired towards lower-fat recipes, this dip is the answer.
It can be made with either light sour cream or plain yogurt.

Makes 1 cup (250 mL)			
I cup	plain yogurt or light sour cream	250 mL
3 tbsp	orange or apple juice	45 mL
I tbsp	liquid honey	15 mL
¼ tsp	ground cinnamon	I mL

1. In a small bowl, stir together yogurt, juice, honey and cinnamon. Cover and refrigerate for up to one week until ready to serve with assorted fresh fruit for dipping.

STRAWBERRIES IN BALSAMIC VINEGAR

You may well wonder about the combination of fruit and balsamic vinegar.
Once you try it, you will understand the magic of the mellow, slightly
sweet flavor of good-quality balsamic vinegar and fruit. Peaches,
strawberries, pitted cherries, blood oranges and grapes are all superb
combinations. Best to use firm fruit so the color does not leach into the syrup.

Serves 4		
3 cups	whole strawberries	750 mL
1½ tbsp	balsamic vinegar	22 mL
2 tbsp	packed brown sugar	25 mL
	Fresh mint leaves, optional	

TIP
Strawberries stop ripening when they're picked. Always choose bright red berries with a sweet smell and no white or green spots.

1. Arrange strawberries in a shallow bowl. Sprinkle with vinegar and sugar. Toss to coat.

2. Let stand at room temperature for up to 30 minutes before serving. Garnish with mint leaves, if using.

LEMON-ROASTED FRUIT

Whether you barbecue, grill or oven-bake fruit, it is a marvelous finale for any dinner party. Try the Ginger Ricotta Cream for a sublime accompaniment to this pineapple recipe.

Serves 6

TIPS

Rum makes a nice replacement for lemon juice.

• PREHEAT OVEN TO 350°F (180°C)
• SHALLOW GLASS BAKING DISH, GREASED

2 tbsp	melted butter or margarine	25 mL
2 tbsp	freshly squeezed lemon juice (see Tip, left)	25 mL
I tbsp	liquid honey	15 mL
3 cups	pineapple chunks, fresh or canned	750 mL
	Fresh mint sprigs, optional	

1. In a medium bowl, combine butter, lemon juice and honey. Toss with pineapple to coat. Let stand at room temperature for 30 minutes or up to 3 hours.

2. Place pineapple in prepared baking dish. Bake in preheated oven for 30 minutes or until fruit is warmed and tender. (The time will differ greatly depending on the fruit you use.) Serve cooked pineapple on individual dessert plates topped with a spoonful of Ginger Ricotta Cream (see recipe, page 170), if desired. Garnish with a mint sprig, if using.

SUGGESTED FRUITS

• I suggest halved fresh or canned fruits, such as peaches, pears, apples or nectarines, pineapple spears, whole strawberries, green or red grapes or black cherries. Add a few slices of papaya or mangoes in season.

CRUSTLESS STRAWBERRY PIE

*Bake this filling with or without a crust. It's about as good as
any strawberry pie filling gets. Serve with a garnish of fresh mint leaves.*

- PREHEAT OVEN TO 350°F (180°C)
- SHALLOW GLASS BAKING DISH OR QUICHE PAN, GREASED

2 cups	quartered strawberries	500 mL
¾ cup	sour cream	175 mL
3	eggs	3
⅔ cup	packed brown sugar	150 mL

1. Arrange strawberries over bottom of prepared baking dish.

2. In a medium bowl, beat together cream, eggs and sugar. Pour over strawberries.

3. Bake for 35 minutes or until filling is set and golden brown.

STRAWBERRIES ROMANOFF

*One of many desserts named by French chefs for Russian nobility, Strawberries
Romanoff is absolutely deliciously decadent. Strawberries are soaked in orange
liqueur or frozen orange juice concentrate and topped with whipped cream.*

Serves 4

TIP
To freeze berries, wash, dry, hull and freeze them in a single layer on a baking sheet. For maximum flavor retention, sprinkle with ¾ cup (175 mL) granulated sugar for every 4 cups (1 L) of fruit. Pack loosely in heavy-duty resealable plastic bags. Date and label bags.

2 cups	strawberries, stems removed and quartered	500 mL
¼ cup	orange liqueur, such as Cointreau	50 mL
3 tbsp	granulated sugar, divided	45 mL
½ cup	chilled whipping (35%) cream	125 mL

1. In a large bowl, toss strawberries with liqueur and 2 tbsp (25 mL) sugar. Set aside at room temperature for 20 minutes, stirring twice.

2. In a small bowl, whip cream with remaining sugar until stiff peaks form. Serve berries with juice and a dollop of whipped cream.

SUMMER FRUIT PARFAIT

Those long hot wonderful days of summer make me seek cool,
soothing light desserts. This parfait is the answer.

Serves 6			
3 cups	prepared fruit such as strawberries, raspberries, blueberries and even sweet cherries		750 mL
1 tbsp	balsamic vinegar		15 mL
1 tbsp	brown or maple sugar		15 mL
1½ cups	yogurt, plain or fruit-flavored		375 mL

1. In a medium bowl, combine prepared fruit, vinegar and sugar. Let stand for 30 minutes to release juices.

2. Spoon fruit mixture into a shallow serving dish. Top with yogurt. Cover and refrigerate for several hours before serving.

SERVING SUGGESTION

- Sprinkle fresh mint leaves, toasted coconut or slivered toasted almonds over the yogurt before serving. Orange or lemon zest adds a nice citrus flavor to the fruit. For single servings, layer fruit and yogurt in parfait glasses.

MELON CONSERVE

A spoonful of this tasty conserve over ice cream or fruit makes a light,
summery dessert. I make it with either cantaloupe or honeydew melon.

Makes 2 cups (500 mL)		
1	large cantaloupe	1
½ cup	granulated sugar	125 mL
2 tbsp	freshly squeezed lemon or lime juice	25 mL
¼ cup	golden raisins	50 mL

Variation
I have also added
preserved ginger
rather than raisins
with excellent results.

1. Peel and seed cantaloupe and cut into bite-size pieces. Set aside.

2. In a large saucepan, bring sugar, $1/4$ cup (50 mL) water and lemon juice to a boil. Boil, uncovered, for 5 minutes.

3. Stir in melon and raisins. Reduce heat and simmer, uncovered, stirring frequently, for 15 minutes or until melon is translucent and syrup thickened. Chill before serving.

GREEK HONEY AND YOGURT

This dessert is as authentic as any served in restaurants in the Plaka in Athens. Fragrant cinnamon sprinkled over yogurt cheese and drizzled with honey makes this an easy, light and low-fat dessert.

Serves 4

TIP
Spread nuts on a pie plate. Bake in 350°F (180°C) oven for about 10 minutes or microwave at High for 5 minutes or until golden. Be careful as nuts toast quickly and can burn easily.

Variation
Rather than pine nuts, you can substitute sliced fresh fruit.

I	Yogurt Cheese (see recipe, page 23)	I
4 tsp	liquid honey	20 mL
Pinch	ground cinnamon	Pinch
4 tsp	toasted pine nuts (see Tip, left)	20 mL

1. Divide yogurt cheese between four dessert dishes. Drizzle each with 1 tsp (5 mL) honey. Refrigerate until serving time.

2. Dust lightly with cinnamon and top each with 1 tsp (5 mL) pine nuts.

CITRUS CHOCOLATE SAUCE

A sauce that combines the flavors of chocolate and orange has to be luscious.

<table>
<tr><td>½ cup</td><td>light (5%) cream</td><td>125 mL</td></tr>
<tr><td>1 tbsp</td><td>corn syrup</td><td>15 mL</td></tr>
<tr><td>3 oz</td><td>semisweet chocolate, chopped</td><td>90 g</td></tr>
<tr><td>1 tbsp</td><td>orange liqueur or frozen orange juice concentrate, thawed</td><td>15 mL</td></tr>
</table>

Makes ¾ cup (175 mL)

TIPS

This make-ahead sauce keeps refrigerated for up to 5 days.

I use this sauce over fresh fruits or for dipping them. And naturally, no dish of ice cream or frozen yogurt would be complete without a good spoonful.

1. In a small saucepan, bring cream and corn syrup to a boil. Add chocolate. Cook, whisking until smooth. Stir in liqueur.

2. Let stand until thickened, about 15 minutes. Refrigerate until ready to use.

LIGHT CHOCOLATE DIP

What a deceptively decadent dip! As well as serving with ice cream and cake, it also makes an excellent chocolate milk drink that children will enjoy.

<table>
<tr><td>1</td><td>can (10 oz/300 mL) low-fat sweetened condensed milk</td><td>1</td></tr>
<tr><td>½ cup</td><td>milk</td><td>125 mL</td></tr>
<tr><td>⅔ cup</td><td>unsweetened cocoa powder</td><td>150 mL</td></tr>
<tr><td>1 tsp</td><td>vanilla extract</td><td>5 mL</td></tr>
</table>

Makes 1½ cups (375 mL)

1. In a microwave-safe bowl, whisk together condensed milk and regular milk. Gradually whisk in cocoa until smooth.

2. Microwave on High for 3 minutes or until bubbly. Stir every 30 seconds. Whisk in vanilla until completely smooth. Serve at once. Store any remaining in refrigerator for up to 3 weeks until ready to use. Heat before serving.

HOT FUDGE SAUCE

This rich sauce is brimming with fine chocolate flavor. Just right for serving over ice cream, frozen yogurt, fruit or a simple cake.

Makes 1 cup (250 mL)			
½ cup	butter or margarine	125 mL
1 cup	semisweet chocolate chips	250 mL
½ cup	corn syrup	125 mL
1 tbsp	rum or brandy or 1 tsp (5 mL) rum or brandy extract	25 mL

1. In a small saucepan, combine butter, chocolate chips and corn syrup. Bring to a boil. Reduce heat and cook slowly until chocolate is melted and mixture is smooth.

2. Remove from heat. Stir in rum. Serve at once. Store any remaining in refrigerator for up to 3 weeks until ready to use. Heat before serving.

EASY CHOCOLATE MOUSSE

Good friend Ruth shared her love of this recipe with me. This silky smooth treat is for chocolate lovers.

Serves 6

TIP
Other flavors than brandy to use are Baileys Irish Cream or rum. If using the Baileys, I generally replace ⅓ cup (75 mL) coffee with Baileys.

• *SIX SMALL CUSTARD CUPS*

1¼ cups	chocolate chips	300 mL
¾ cup	strong coffee	175 mL
¼ cup	milk	50 mL
1 tbsp	brandy or 1 tsp (5 mL) brandy extract	15 mL
	Sweetened whipped cream, optional	

1. Place chocolate chips in blender.

2. Heat coffee and milk to steaming (see Tip, left). Pour into blender. Process with chocolate until smooth and creamy.

3. Add brandy. Pour into six very small custard cups. Refrigerate until chilled.

4. At serving time, top with a dollop of whipped cream, if using.

CHOCOLATE SOUFFLÉ

No one will guess this marvelously sophisticated dessert has only four ingredients.

Serves 4	

TIP

Soufflés can be assembled up to 30 minutes before baking and kept at room temperature. Cover with an inverted bowl, being careful it does not touch top of soufflé.

• *PREHEAT OVEN TO 375°F (190°C)*
• *4-CUP (1 L) SOUFFLÉ DISH, LIGHTLY GREASED*

½ cup	granulated sugar, divided	125 mL
5 oz	bittersweet chocolate, chopped	150 g
3	egg yolks, beaten	3
6	egg whites	6
Pinch	salt	Pinch

1. Sprinkle a small amount of sugar in prepared soufflé dish.

2. In a small bowl, melt chocolate over barely simmering water. Stir occasionally until smooth. Remove bowl from heat. Whisk in beaten egg yolks (watch as mixture will thicken).

3. In a small bowl, beat egg whites and salt with an electric mixer until soft peaks form. Add remaining sugar, a little at a time. Continue beating at medium speed until stiff peaks form. Stir about 1 cup (250 mL) whites into chocolate mixture (this will lighten chocolate). Then gently fold in remaining whites.

4. Spoon into prepared soufflé dish. Bake in preheated oven for 24 minutes or until puffed and crusted on top but not quite set in center. Serve immediately.

BROWN SUGAR RUM GLAZE

This easy-to-make and very flavorful glaze will "dress" the most humble cake. Try it over angel food, chocolate or spice cake or ice cream.

Makes ⅓ cup (75 mL)	

¼ cup	lightly packed brown sugar	50 mL
3 tbsp	butter or margarine	45 mL
1 tbsp	dark rum	15 mL
⅓ cup	confectioner's (icing) sugar, sifted	75 mL

TIP
This makes sufficient glaze for one 10 oz (300 g) prepared or store-bought angel food cake.

1. In a microwave-safe container, heat brown sugar and butter on High for 1 minute or until mixture is bubbly. Whisk in rum and confectioner's sugar until smooth.

2. Pour the glaze over your favorite cake, allowing it to run down the sides. Let stand for 20 minutes or until glaze firms up before serving.

GANACHE SOUFFLÉ IN CHOCOLATE CUPS

Add a small amount of brandy or fruit liqueur to a rich chocolate/heavy cream icing and you will be amazed to produce such an elegant dessert so easily.

Serves 10

TIPS
As to be expected, the cream-chocolate mixture turns a light brown while beating.

Use the best quality chocolate you can find. The better the chocolate, the better the finished dessert will taste.

- *12-CUP MUFFIN PAN, 10 LINED WITH PAPER CUPS*
- *(FILL REMAINING TWO CUPS WITH WATER)*

8 oz	semisweet chocolate, chopped	250 g
1 cup	whipping (35%) cream	250 mL
10 oz	milk chocolate, chopped	300 g
2 tbsp	brandy	25 mL

1. *To make cups:* Place semisweet chocolate in top of a double boiler over hot but not boiling water. Stir constantly until chocolate is smooth and melted.

2. Spoon 1 tbsp (15 mL) melted chocolate into each paper liner. With a pastry brush, coat bottom and sides of liners evenly with chocolate. Freeze for 30 minutes or until chocolate hardens. Repeat with remaining chocolate. Freeze again.

3. *To make ganache soufflé:* In a large saucepan over medium heat bring cream almost to a boil. Remove from heat. Add milk chocolate pieces. Cover and let stand for 5 minutes until chocolate softens. Stir until smooth. Transfer mixture to a large bowl and refrigerate until cold. Beat with an electric mixer on medium speed for 3 minutes or until fluffy. Gradually mix in brandy.

4. Peel paper liners from chocolate cups and spoon ganache into each. Best to serve immediately.

CAPPUCCINO DESSERT SPECIALTY

You'll be a hero to the coffee lovers in your life when you serve this custard dessert.

Serves 6		

TIP
A dollop of whipped cream provides the perfect finish.

¼ cup	cornstarch	50 mL
3 cups	milk, divided	750 mL
I cup	granulated sugar	250 mL
2 tbsp	instant coffee granules	25 mL
¼ tsp	salt	I mL

1. In a small bowl, whisk cornstarch and ¼ cup (50 mL) milk until smooth. Set aside.

2. In a large heavy saucepan, combine sugar, coffee granules and salt. Whisk in ⅔ cup (150 mL) hot water. Cook over medium heat, stirring constantly, for 4 minutes or until mixture comes to a boil. Stir in remaining milk.

3. Add reserved cornstarch mixture to hot coffee mixture. Reduce heat and cook slowly for 10 minutes or until mixture bubbles and is smooth and thickened.

4. Divide coffee mixture among six dessert dishes. Cover and refrigerate until chilled for up to 2 days.

ICE CREAM PIE

Almost any pie is a great dessert but an ice cream one can be made ahead, then frozen to use at a later time. When my 11-year-old granddaughters were visiting, they made this recipe frequently. As you can imagine, it did not last long.

Serves 6 to 8		

• 9-INCH (23 CM) SPRINGFORM PAN, GREASED

¼ cup	granulated sugar	50 mL
I ½ cups	crisp rice cereal, partially crushed	375 mL
3 tbsp	finely grated bittersweet chocolate, divided	45 mL
3 cups	ice cream, any favorite flavor, slightly softened	750 mL

1. In a heavy saucepan, cook sugar slowly on low heat until it begins to melt. Continue to cook, stirring occasionally, for 3 minutes or until it turns into a deep caramel color.

2. Remove pan from heat, then immediately stir in cereal. Quickly transfer to prepared springform pan. Spread evenly over bottom and smooth top with back of a small spoon.

3. Sprinkle 2 tbsp (25 mL) chocolate over warm crust to melt. Then spread chocolate with back of spoon over crust.

4. Spoon ice cream over crust. Sprinkle with remaining chocolate. Cover and freeze.

5. Remove from freezer at serving time. Run a sharp knife around edge of crust and remove sides of pan. Cut into wedges to serve.

ICE CREAM AND BERRIES

Choose two of your favorite flavors of ice cream, add your favorite berry and either a caramel or Citrus Chocolate Sauce. What a winner and soooo easy!

Serves 6	• 9-BY 5-INCH (2 L) LOAF PAN, LINED WITH PLASTIC WRAP		
	2 cups	each of two of your favorite ice cream	500 mL
	2 cups	sliced strawberries or whole raspberries	500 mL
	2	kiwi fruit, peeled and chopped	2
		Citrus Chocolate Sauce (see recipe, page 176), optional	

1. Allow ice cream to soften at room temperature.

2. Spread one flavor of ice cream into prepared pan, pressing down firmly. Press second ice cream over first. Cover with plastic wrap and return to freezer to firm up.

3. Invert loaf pan onto a serving plate. Remove plastic wrap and cut into thin slices. Serve with prepared fruits and a drizzle of sauce, if using.

ICE CREAM DESSERT WITH BALSAMIC SYRUP

Two layers of ice cream topped with a meringue and a drizzle of Balsamic Syrup make a large and very flavorful dessert. Perfect for a crowd!

Serves 12

TIP

Any combination of flavors works well in this dessert. Sometimes, I use three or four thinner layers of ice cream. If you can find pistachio or lemon, they are marvelous additions.

• 9-INCH (23 CM) SPRINGFORM PAN

2 cups	each chocolate and vanilla ice cream (see Tip, left)	500 mL
4	egg whites, at room temperature	4
¼ cup	granulated sugar	50 mL
	Fresh fruits and mint sprigs for garnish, optional	
	Balsamic Syrup (see recipe, page 183)	

1. Allow chocolate ice cream to soften at room temperature. Spread into bottom of pan. Cover and freeze until solid.

2. Repeat process with vanilla ice cream, making two distinct layers. Cover and freeze.

3. Preheat broiler. In a medium bowl, beat egg whites with an electric mixer on medium speed until soft peaks form. Increase speed to high, gradually adding sugar. Beat until shiny stiff peaks have formed. Spread meringue over top of ice cream.

4. Broil until golden brown. Let cool. Cover and freeze until firm.

5. At serving time, remove sides from pan. Cut frozen dessert into slices. Garnish each serving with fruit and mint leaves, if using. Drizzle with Balsamic Syrup.

BALSAMIC SYRUP

*Balsamic vinegar, sugar and water create this absolutely amazing syrup.
I try to always keep some on hand to serve with ice creams, frozen yogurts,
fresh fruits or even for sweet pancakes or waffles. It is important
that you use a good-quality balsamic vinegar.*

Makes ½ cup (125 mL)		
½ cup	granulated sugar	125 mL
2 tbsp	balsamic vinegar	25 mL

1. In a small saucepan, combine sugar and ¼ cup (50 mL) water. Bring to a boil over medium heat until sugar dissolves. Remove from heat and stir in vinegar. Set aside to cool. Store in a tightly covered container in the refrigerator.

LEMON CREAM CURD

*Tart and tangy, lemon curd is a multi-purpose and very versatile filling. It is easy
and fast to prepare using a microwave oven. Serve it over fresh fruits, use as a base for
lemon pie or a filling for miniature tarts. And it is always a wake-up call on waffles.*

Makes 1 cup (250 mL)		
2	lemons	2
¼ cup	butter or margarine	50 mL
¾ cup	granulated sugar	175 mL
2	eggs, beaten	2

TIPS

Do not allow the mixture to boil as it will curdle. It thickens during cooling.

To lighten the curd for a pie filling, fold in whipped cream or, for a lighter filling, fold in plain yogurt.

1. Finely grate lemon zest. (You should have about 2 tbsp/25 mL.) Squeeze lemons and measure ½ cup (125 mL) juice. Place in 4-cup (1 L) microwave-safe container. Whisk in zest, butter and sugar.

2. Microwave on High for 1½ minutes or until butter is melted. Whisk in beaten eggs until well mixed.

3. Return to microwave and cook on Medium for 2 minutes, stirring every 30 seconds or until mixture is thickened. Let cool. Store in a covered container in the refrigerator for up to 2 weeks or freeze for longer storage.

TOFU RUM PUDDING

Extra firm tofu provides the best texture and flavor for this delicious dessert.
And no one will guess it has tofu. It takes on the rum flavor.

Serves 6		

1 cup	packed brown sugar	250 mL
⅔ cup	dark rum	150 mL
3 tbsp	butter or margarine	45 mL
Pinch	salt	Pinch
1 lb	extra firm tofu, drained	500 g

Variation
You can use rum extract instead of the dark rum. Increase water to 1 cup (250 mL).

1. In a small saucepan, combine sugar, rum, ½ cup (125 mL) water, butter and salt. Bring to a boil. Reduce heat and simmer for 10 minutes or until mixture is reduced to 1 cup (250 mL).

2. Place drained tofu in food processor or blender. With motor running, slowly add hot rum until mixture is smooth. Pour into six serving dishes. Cover and refrigerate for 4 hours or until set.

TOFU CHOCOLATE MOUSSE

Thick, rich and creamy, this incredible tasting
lightened chocolate mousse demands you take bite after bite!
This version has become one of my favorite ways to impress guests.

Serves 6		

½ cup	semisweet chocolate chips, melted	125 mL
10 oz	firm tofu, drained	300 g
⅓ cup	granulated sugar	75 mL
2	egg whites	2
Pinch	salt	Pinch

SAFETY TIP
Pouring hot syrup over beaten egg whites brings them to a safe serving temperature that is sufficient to kill harmful bacteria.

1. In a food processor or blender, process melted chocolate chips and tofu until smooth.

2. In a small saucepan, boil sugar and 3 tbsp (45 mL) water until a candy thermometer reads 238°F (115°C), about 5 minutes.

3. Meanwhile, in a small bowl, beat egg whites and salt with an electric mixer on high until stiff peaks form.

4. In a thin steady stream, pour hot syrup over beaten whites. Beat at high speed until stiff peaks form (see Safety Tip, below left). Stir one-quarter of meringue into chocolate mixture. Fold in remaining meringue.

5. Evenly divide mousse into six small dishes. Cover and refrigerate for at least 4 hours before serving.

COCONUT DESSERT CHEESE

Dress up a cheese ball with icing sugar, orange liqueur and coconut and suddenly you have a dessert. It keeps well in the refrigerator or in the freezer for longer storage.

Serves 8			
8 oz	cream cheese, softened	250 g
½ cup	confectioner's (icing) sugar, sifted	125 mL
2 tbsp	orange liqueur such as Cointreau, Grand Marnier or Curacao	25 mL
½ cup	sweetened dessicated coconut	125 mL

1. In a small bowl, with an electric mixer, beat cream cheese, sugar and liqueur until smooth. Form into a ball. Roll ball in coconut until well coated. Refrigerate for several days or freeze for longer storage.

2. Serve at room temperature with cut up fresh fruits and a simple cookie or gingersnaps.

Library and Archives Canada Cataloguing in Publication

Howard, Margaret, 1930–
The 250 best 4-ingredient recipes / Margaret Howard.

Includes index.
ISBN 978-0-7788-0066-8

1. Quick and easy cookery. I. Title. II. Title: Two hundred fifty best four-ingredient recipes.

TX833.5.H69 2009   641.5'55   C2008-907688-5

INDEX